Daddy's Wives
By: Rose Arrington

SH Management & Publishing Group, LLC

2476 Nimmo Parkway
Suite 115/#232
Virginia Beach, VA 23456

vizhun75@gmail.com

ISBN 978-0-9834912-5-5

First Printing October 2010
Revised Edition Printing April 2021

Printed in United States of America

Cover Designed by Jimi Dantzler

Editing by Reid2Right Writing & Editing

Dedication

For all the young girls and boys who lost their innocence before time yet, maintained hope and strength by the grace of God. Keep fighting through the trials and tribulations. Keep living by faith. This book stands as a testimony, inspired by knowing we can do all things through Christ who strengthens us.

Acknowledgements

I want to first thank Jesus Christ for his strength and guidance to complete this book. The journey into my past was painful, but on this spiritual walk with God, He allowed me to come across many people who cried with me, listened to me, and cared about me. You know who you are, thank you! I extend my sincere gratitude and all my love to you.

Table of Contents

Girl, I Used to Know

As I lay asleep in my queen size bed.
I hear the sworn soft whisper of the girl I used to
know.
She was hurting, a heartbreaking cry.
Asking for help, screaming for God.
I couldn't really recognize this girl,
she had open wounds, mud-stained clothes, but she
used to be me.
As I walked to her in my cotton white gown.
I had to think and ask myself, what can I do to heal
this girl?
What could I do to ensure she was safe?
The girl I used to know; she fell to her knees.
She opened her heart, she had large tears on her
cheeks.
He ruined my life; he took my innocence.
He destroyed my childhood, who am I now with this?
I could see the pain in her eyes, I could hear the hurt
in her cries.
I wish I could tell her everything will be alright.
I got on one knee; I wiped her last tear.
I took a deep breath, and I faced my last fear.
Dear girl I used to know; beauty is within.
He did not destroy you; he just gave your mind a
spin.
For God is the healer, the protector of your life.
You can still be a woman; you can still be a wife.
Look at me now, your past doesn't define you.

You have to be thankful for good things around you.
You have to see the good inside you, and you have to
leave all the past events behind you.
Beauty is within, I know this now.
And I have to thank you, the girl I used to know.
I picked the girl up; I closed her sore wounds.
I gave her a white gown, and told her what to do.

Pick your head up, chest out, smile large, God is the
creator, and you are fine the way you are!

Written by Shaniya "Tootsie Marie" Artis ~
granddaughter of Rose Arrington

Tiffany's Story

Let me tell you about a girl named Tiffany.
She was 16 and pregnant, her life seemed in infamy.
Her life went left when she lost her virginity.
Mind you she's a church girl & sin is just a sin to me.

Tiffany was broke struggling in the slums of the city.
Her mom was never home she was clubbing getting litty.
Her stepdad was always in the house acting silly.
Cause when her mom leaves, he's just trying to touch her kitty.

Tiffany was molested at the age of 13.
And she can't go to her mom about the entire thing.
See her mom's named Kennedy, and Kennedy was abused.
Her husband was the master he created all the rules.

Her mom feels that something's wrong,
but what can she do?
Cause if Kennedy speaks, he will attack her in the room.

Tiffany runs to church to just get away from the madness.
She's praying to baby Jesus and telling him what's been happening.
Tiffany's also gifted so she's writing and she rapping.

But if her stepdad found out he'll have a fit.
Cause in Tiffany's raps she has the power to spit.
She's calling Tim a bastard and she's saying that he's a bitch.
She's got so much anger in her heart that she might flip.

Knowing that it's a baby in her stomach she's always stressed.
Her mother's always too drunk to let her get it off her chest.
Her stepdad had some shots so he's just tryna touch her chest.

But Tiffany can't tolerate the family it's a mess.
So, Tiffany found a rope and she had an idea in mind.
So, Tiffany hung herself and left a suicide note behind.

On the bed and it read:

"God, please help Tim forgive the sins in the bed. God, please save my kid from the scenes in my head. I was 13 and my heart was already dead.

Mother, I tried to tell you, but you were clouded with all the liquor. And God please forgive Tim for every time he hit her. Give mother the strength to use time to reconsider, I'll still be right here with you."

Goodbye ...

Written by Shaniya "Tootsie Marie" Artis
~ granddaughter of Rose Arrington

PROLOGUE

It was a warm, bright, and sunny day in May. A beautiful day when you wake up to birds singing and a rushing cool breeze flowing through the bedroom window. I hear my granddaughter, Jada, singing down the hall as she practices her graduation march. We smile, my daughter, Alexis and I, as she urges us to hurry and get dressed for her big event. Jada wants to be on time to her preschool graduation. I can only imagine it's one of the biggest days in the mind of a young child. I know it is for me.

As we pull into the parking lot of Lakeland Elementary School, Jada is so happy to see her friends. All of them, adorned in their graduation outfits, look so adorable and grown up. She calls out to them and with her mom's loving smile and motherly nod of approval she joins them as they enter the auditorium.

The unconditional affection for our children filled the room with energy and life, chattering and hugging one another as we surveyed the room for good seats. We found good seats on the third row, near the end. Far enough to see Jada, close enough for her to see us. I look around the room filled with loved ones; mothers, fathers, grandparents, friends and notice my granddaughter's class appear in the doorway. They're the first class to march. My heart jumps with excitement and joy, directing Alexis to take pictures, lots of pictures of my granddaughter standing in line.

I take a moment to admire how delightful my Jada has turned out to be. She is beautiful with her pretty pink dress, white shoes, and pink and white socks, and her hair adorning a single white flower tucked into her bun. Alexis stands to take the first shot as the class marches in on "Pomp and Circumstance". Their little feet on beat as lights flash from cameras of family and friends standing in chairs to capture this unforgettable moment.

Everyone is cheering and clapping as Jada and her classmates walk proudly down the aisle. As she turns toward the stage, I see her smiling face, so mature, so innocent.

At five years old she is marching to the beat like a college graduate with her head held high. All her classmates are walking in a single line as if they are walking the red carpet of the Dolby Theatre for an Oscar. I became overwhelmed with emotion and tears began to run down my face as my mind took me back to when I was five. My tears flowed heavily, and my heart began to ache as I recalled myself forty-five years earlier crying and hurting. As I cried, my mind was telling me to run but I couldn't move. My mind became a time machine travelling from the past to the present until I heard people clapping.

I come to, remembering it's my granddaughter's day, her graduation day. She worked hard and practiced long for this day. When I saw her on stage, I could tell she was looking for us, so I waved, and she waved back with such peace and reassurance in her eyes.

The teacher began to pass out awards as each name is called. All the children stood up and walked across the stage to receive their award and bow to us to receive their praise. My heart is overjoyed for them. When Jada walks across the stage, she receives her award and to everyone's surprise she turns to the audience and yells, "Thanks, mom". The auditorium is filled with laughter and loud applause. I smile as my heart is filled with joy, but a sadness overtakes me as my mind begins to fill with thoughts of my childhood.

"Dear God, please give me the strength to hold back this awful pain and hurt I am feeling. Please Lord, not now. Let it be later when I can deal with it."

After the ceremony we all say our goodbyes and go for dinner at one of Jada's favorite restaurants. She shouts, "Captain Lobsters & Seafood!" Oh, how she loves seafood, especially lobsters. She always took them home even though her mother eventually threw them away.

Throughout dinner, she goes on and on about her graduation day. It was a blessing to see her happy and smiling again since her grandfather passed of a heart attack back in January. She loved him dearly and was home with him the morning he died. For such a young child, she was strong, my rock during this time and had assured her "Orlando", which she always called him, was in Heaven and he was alright because he was with God. Today she is bursting with joy and I cannot help but to be happy for her. She shows her awards to the waiter and to our surprise they bring her a cupcake with a candle. Jada giggles as she hugs the waiter and graces her mother and I with kisses. Soon after, Alexis shares another surprise, a trip to the movies to see the new Disney film Jada spoke so highly about. And just like before, she asks the waiter to pack up her lobster shell to take home. As we prepare to leave, she walks around the table and gives me a long, hard hug, "Grandma, I love you", she says. I needed to hear those words. "I love you, too."

As I watch them leave the restaurant a strange feeling overwhelms me, disconnecting me from the moment. Today was the first time in my whole life that the little girl inside me was crying to come out. She needed to talk, to say so many things that she could never say before. I immediately got up from the table and left to go home. As soon as I walked in the door, I removed my shoes, changed my clothes, and decided to write down what I was feeling. I needed to write down what was crying to come out of me all day. After two hours of writing, I got up to stretch my legs and make a cup of coffee. My mind began to play my past like an old black and white movie, so I went back to the computer to continue my story.

CHAPTER ONE

The Meeting

"So be strong and courageous! Do not be afraid and do not panic before them. For the Lord your God will personally go ahead of you. He will neither fail you nor abandon you."

Deuteronomy 31:6 New Living Translation (NLT)

I could see myself, Rose, a four-year-old little girl playing outdoors, jumping rope on a hot sunny day. Oh, it was such a lovely day, and I was such a pretty little girl, two long ponytails, with colorful ribbons, and a cute face with a smile that went from ear to ear. I was very short with fat little legs, like my momma. On this day I was dressed in a white dress that seemed to blow and move with the wind. I looked like an angel. I was so happy and carefree at this age. I loved playing with my dolls and sharing with my sister. We would make mud pies and set up play stores to sell leaves and rocks to my brothers. I loved the sunrise in the early mornings, I loved getting up with my mama and looking at the night's sky filled with the shining stars, I loved when my mom would take us in after playing late outdoors. I loved everybody! I loved life!

My thoughts took me back to when I was a child and we lived at 1307 Macon Street, which was my grandparents' house. It was a big house with two stories and was painted white with green trimmings. There was a very large back porch and when you opened the door there was this large kitchen where I remember eating some of the best soul food I have ever tasted. The next room was the den with grandpa's leather recliner sofa and big radio. Grandpa was always playing the radio with a preacher preaching or religious music.

To the right of the living room was a bedroom; straight ahead was another large bedroom that led to the front room. From the front room, there were a set of stairs that led to the four bedrooms on the second floor. There was a large screened in porch with a green swing that all the children loved to play on. Only three of us could sit in the swing at a time, but we took turns. There was this huge peach tree in the back yard, and in the summer, my grandpa would let us pick peaches from his peach tree, and we would eat until our stomachs hurt.

My grandmother would sometimes make peach cobbler, which was delicious. Sometimes she would preserve them, and they would end up being the best jam in town. I can almost taste that peach jam on some of grandma's homemade hot biscuits right out of the oven.

My mother, Maureen Oakes, was married to a Marine Staff Sergeant whom I saw only once in my life and never as a child. He was always gone, always out to sea for months and months. My mother told us that our father's name was Darnell William Oakes, and she had borne him four children, my two brothers, Darnell Jr. and Greg, my sister Tracy, and me.

My mother, Maureen Oakes, was the baby of her mother, Ruby Wright and Walley Wright. She was her mother's favorite child and she always did as she pleased. As a young woman, she was very promiscuous. Because of her wild lifestyle her parents sent her to New Jersey to live with her oldest brother and his wife, hoping to change her ways. She did the same in New Jersey, so her brother sent her back to Wakefield, North Carolina. It was there she met and married Darnell William Oakes. While he was out to sea, Maureen still lived the nightlife.

We moved out of my grandparents' home into a spacious four-bedroom house on Coventry Road. The house was white with green shutters, a pretty white picket fence, green grass, and yellow sunflowers that grew tall. In the summer our house stayed cool with air conditioning and during the winter it was nice and warm throughout the house. It was pleasant living there with its wide backyard and trees my brothers loved to climb. Then one day we moved from this big house in an affluent neighborhood into a small shoddy old apartment over my grandparents' garage. As soon as I walked up the raggedy stairs made of rotten wood, I knew I wouldn't like living here. The place smelled old and musty. It had one small living room, a bedroom, a tiny kitchen, and an old wood stove stood in the middle of the front room that burned bright red once hot. When it stormed, the lightning rocked the entire house like a rocking chair. Life wasn't easy living over my grandparents' garage. Mama kept a nice, clean home for me and my siblings, but it was nothing like the house on Coventry Road. Our backyard was a trainyard and during the day we watched the trains pull into the yard to load up coal and at night we could hear the train pulling in boxcars full of coal. Things seemed to get worse as mama began to make decisions that negatively affected all our lives.

I remember the day mama met her lifelong boyfriend. It changed my life and ended my childhood. One hot summer morning mama got us up and ready. She dressed my brothers in short sets with bow ties and white shoes. My sister and I wore cute dresses with starched slips that scratched our legs as we walked in our white buckled shoes. Mama put on her beautiful pink dress with the pink belt and her white high heel shoes to show off her legs. And as always, she smelled sweet like roses.

As we walked downtown on 17th Street, me and my sister held hands, my brothers held hands, and mama walked behind us. When we walked into this barbershop with the spinning red and white pole mama told us to sit together and be quiet. Three barber chairs lined up on a real shiny floor and a big fan over our heads turned slowly as two men inside the shop cut hair. Hair clippers hung on the side of their desk with glass bottles of green liquid and mirrors everywhere. Mama looked out the door and saw Ms. Veronica, one of her friends. She told us to sit still so she could go speak to Ms. Veronica and as mama stood up and walked to the door, the twist in her hip caught the eye of one of the barbers. Even as she stood outside talking, this man continued to watch her. Once he finished cutting hair, he washed his hands and went outside to talk to mama and Ms. Veronica and joined them laughing. When mama and this man came back into the shop, he cut my brother's, Darnell, hair first. Then he cut Greg's hair and mama stood by him and watched his every move. They kept talking and smiling at one another, gazing into each other's eyes. When he finished cutting my brother's hair, mama wrote something on a piece of paper the barber gave her and walked him over to us. His name was Luther Cornell Yates, Jr., a light-skinned man with a gold tooth and scary looking green eyes. He was the owner of the barbershop and owned real estate with dreams of becoming a millionaire someday.

Later in life I found out Luther Cornell Yates, Jr. was born in Macon, Virginia to Eva and Luther Cornell Yates, Sr. whom he addressed as mama and papa. As the seventh of ten children, he considered himself blessed. He quit school at an early age to work on his papa's farm. Life on the farm was very poor, so after he worked the fields during the day, he cut hair in the evenings. He learned to cut hair on an old stump in the backyard and according to him, people came from miles around and waited all day for a haircut by this gifted boy. Luther wanted to be rich and famous so at the age of 18 he left his papa's farm in Macon and moved to the city with only ten cents in his pocket.

After a while we left so mama could take care of some business. Mr. Yates gave each of us a dollar, so we stopped at the nickel and dime store, Woolworth's, for toys. Me and my sister bought a jump rope and bobby jacks, and the boys bought a bag of marbles and a small ball. On our way down 17th street mama asked a photographer to take our photo. We all sat beside each other, girls on the right, boys on the left, as he told us to smile. After our impromptu photo session mama treated us to an ice cream cone then we all got into a cab to go home.

That evening she was smiling and singing as she was prepared dinner. After feeding us and getting us ready for bed, she started to dress. I sat in the corner of the front room and just watched her as she prepared herself for this date. She was a pretty lady with smooth, pecan brown skin. I always loved to watch her as she put on her stockings. First, she would roll them down in her hands then hold out one leg and pull them up until she reached the garter. Then, she would put out the other leg and do the same. The stockings looked so nice on her legs. When I rubbed up against them, they were silky and soft. Her hair was long and black, and she would always style it in an upsweep. Mama was stunning and looked good in everything she wore.

Once she was dressed, she stood in front of the mirror and twirled so she could see how nice she looked.

There was a knock on the door, it was my Uncle Max. He came over to babysit us while mama was out on her date. She told us all to go to bed as she rushed out the door. I looked around the corner of the room as she reached back into the door to grab her purse. I tiptoed out the room into the front room and looked out the window. There was a big, shiny, blue car parked in the driveway. A man opened the car door for her, and he was grinning from ear to ear. Then I saw it, the gold tooth, shining. I knew exactly who it was, the man from the barbershop, who cut my brothers' hair earlier that day, Mister Luther Cornell Yates Jr. As I gazed at his tooth, my Uncle Max was coming up the stairs, so I quickly ran back to my room and jumped in the bed.

After that night, mama and Mr. Yates hung out a lot. My uncle kept us night after night and sometimes overnight when mama didn't come home until the morning. She started bringing bags of new expensive clothes to wear on her dates. He even bought her jewelry and nice smelling perfumes.

This went on forever and it seemed mama no longer had time for us. In the mornings she was on the phone making plans to be with him that evening, and so we were left another night without her. Shortly, after those nights out, mama started getting sick. She would throw up all the time and lay in the bed most of the day. I noticed her stomach was getting big and it looked like she was gaining weight. The light-skinned barber, Mr. Yates, started coming over more often. He would come in our house and walk up our stairs.

One day, when we came home from school, mama wasn't there. Grandma told us mama went to the hospital to have a baby and she would keep us until mama returned home. Mama gave birth to a little girl and named her Heather Annette Oakes. In about three days she came home with this baby wrapped in a beautiful pink blanket. Even though she was Luther's baby, her last name was Oakes like ours. Mama was still married to my father; Darnell W. Oakes and she used his Marine medical benefits for the doctor and hospital expenses for having the baby. Heather, my new sister, was mama's and Mr. Yates first child together.

The evening mama bought Heather home, I walked over to her crib in the living room and pulled the blanket back. I saw a little light baby crying and she looked almost white, like Mr. Yates. When I turned around, he was standing there with those scary green eyes reaching out to grab me. I started twisting and turning my body to get from his grip. He had this real sneaky laugh that I can hear in my head even now. Then he said,

"You see my baby, ain't she pretty?"

"Look at me!"

I took one look and as soon as he put me down, I ran out the room. Ever since the baby was born, he was always at the house. One day he bought his brother, Gordon, over to see Heather.

"What about your wife and children you have at home?" Gordan asked. Mr. Yates replied haughtily,

"I am a Muslim; my religion will allow me to have as many wives as I can and as long as I financially take care of them then there is no problem."

"Remember lil' bro, I am the boss, I got this under control!"

I found out later mama knew the barber was married with children. He was married to Joann Reid Yates and they had six children. Joann knew that L.C. (his nickname) was seeing a woman in Wakefield and apparently mama met L.C. before our trip to the barbershop. They met at a nightclub, where he played in a band, and she was fine with being his mistress.

Before she started seeing Mr. Yates, mama had time for us. She played with us, took us to the movies, and treated us to popcorn and ice cream. But now, from the time she got up in the morning until the time we went to bed, she would take every opportunity to leave us and go to him. The house was always cold, and we did not appear to have a lot of money. However, back then me and my siblings were close, so we had each other.

Summer of 1956, mama took us around the corner from my grandparents' house to pull up weeds and clean up the yard. There was so much debris and wild roots to pull up, it seemed like we would never finish. While we were working, L.C. told us this was where he was going to build mama a house. He said our new house would have three bedrooms, a large kitchen, a bathroom, a living room, and a porch. I was so happy because it sounded like the house we had moved from before we moved in the apartment over my grandparents' garage. Now, my brothers won't have to hide under the steps until their school friends left so they could come up the stairs. He called us all together and told us he was our Daddy, and we were to call him *"Daddy"*. He even told my mama, to call him Daddy, too, and she did.

Within the next few weeks, Daddy started construction on the lot to build us a house as he had promised. Mama would have us up late at night while she was painting and cleaning. We all would fall asleep in the house because she would work late to get the house ready. Within six months the house was complete, and we moved in. It was a nice house and I remember you could walk through the back door into the kitchen. The next room was the dining room, and then the living room which led to the front porch. You had to walk through the dining room to the bedrooms. Mama's room was facing the dining room and then down the hall to the left was the girl's room and to the right was my brother's room. Daddy came to the house every night once the house was complete. He would close the barbershop and come by the house until late. He never slept over. Even though I was only five, I was aware of the major changes taking place in my life.

Soon enough, Daddy became the "King of the castle." Mama addressed him as such from time to time. I realized he was taking over when he started eating at the house. He made up a rule for us to not eat until he ate. Mama made sure we followed it. We had to come, sit down, and watch Daddy eat, and then when he was finished, we could eat. Mama made him number one and we had to do whatever he asked. Our responsibility was to serve him without question. It was obvious my mother had fallen deeply in love with this man.

Another rule was for all the girls to greet him "properly" with a kiss, not on the cheeks, but directly on the mouth. We had to kiss him on the mouth every time he came home and when he left. As a five-year-old girl, I did not want to kiss any man, especially on the mouth. I hated kissing him and greeting this man I had to call Daddy, but mama insisted, so I had no choice.

When he came home in the morning, I would run and hide, but mama would call my name and make me come and kiss him. Through my body language I made it clear that I did not want to kiss him. I would cry and after I kissed him, she would send me to my room. When Daddy left for the barbershop, Mama would argue and fuss and sometimes even beat me for my behavior. So, I learned early on that if I did not want any beatings, I had to obey.

CHAPTER TWO

A Child's Nightmare Begins

"Lord, when doubts fill my mind, when my heart is in turmoil, quiet me and give me renewed hope and cheer."

Psalm 94:19 Living Bible (TLB)

L.C. would take us all out in his shiny big car at night to get ice cream at Bentleys' Ice Cream on 17th Street. My mother was up front holding Heather and in the back seat, I sat between my brothers while my sister sat by the door. When we finished our ice cream, Daddy drove us around for a while or until we fell asleep.

One night he told mama he was only taking me for ice cream. My sister Tracy cried when I left because she wanted to go too. I got into the car and sat close to the passenger door.

"Don't be afraid," he said, *"I'm not going to hurt you. Come, sit on my lap and I will let you drive."*

He had that big ole smile that I hated so much, but I wanted to drive, so I got in his lap began to turn the wheel right then left pretending I was really driving. We went on Main Street and passed my grandparents' house on Randolph Avenue.

I was enjoying this game until I could feel his hand under my dress and in my underwear. He put his finger in my vagina and I jumped out of his lap and moved toward the door. I was so afraid. He stopped the car and unzipped his pants. He pulled me closer to him, grabbed my hand and put it on his penis, telling me to move my hands up and down. I wanted to jump out of the car and run but my body wouldn't move. I started to cry but he didn't care. He kept on saying,

"Move your hands harder and harder until I tell you to stop."

Then I felt something wet on my hand, there was cum all over the front seat of the car. He got out of the car and went to the truck, when he came back, he had a cloth and used it to wipe my hands off and clean the front seat.

Afterwards, he took me to High's Ice Cream Parlor, and I cried all the way there. I didn't stop crying even when I got home. I jumped out the car and ran into the house crying. He told mama I had been a bad girl and wouldn't stop crying. Mama became angry with me and sent me straight to my room, she told me I was not going to get any ice cream since I didn't know how to act. She later came into the room and punished me by beating me with his belt. She sent me straight to bed and told me that I was a bad girl for making Daddy mad.

When I got up the next morning, Mama was in the kitchen cooking and I remember trying to explain to her what took place the night before. My mother became very angry with me and told me to shut up. She called me a liar and told me if she ever heard me say anything like that about Daddy, she would beat me twice as hard and send me away.

On several other occasions after that night, Daddy tried to take me for a ride alone in the car, but I would start to cry, and he would send me to bed and take my sister. She would come back crying too. Mama was always mad because he fussed at her when we cried.

One-night mama was getting all the children ready to go to the movies. Daddy wasn't feeling well and told mama he didn't want to go. Then he told her that I shouldn't go because I'd been a bad girl crying and lying on him. He said I should stay home with the baby as punishment so that I would learn that I must obey him. Of course, my mother agreed with him and made me stay home.

Once they left the house for the movies, I went to my room to play. I was changing their clothes and talking to them when suddenly, he came into my room. My heart began to beat faster as he came closer.

It was like I could hear my heart beating outside my little chest, but I didn't want to cry. I was already being punished for crying. As I looked up, he was sitting on the bed beside me. I began to move away from him, but he just slid over, put his hands under my gown, pulled my panties down, and felt my vagina with his fingers. He unzipped his pants, pulled his penis out, and climbed on top of me. He started to rub my private with his penis and I started to cry. It seemed like I was crying loud, but I realized it was just my voice crying in my head. I was too scared to cry out. Then it happened. He pushed his penis inside of me with great force. I immediately felt intense pain and began to cry out loud so he could hear me, but he didn't care. He pushed in and out as his large body was over me, sweat rolling off his body unto my gown. He began to moan then came on me, the bed and my gown. I didn't know what else to do but cry and lay there while he got off me.

I could hear the water running continuously. Then the bathroom door opened, and he came out with a wet, cold washcloth that he used to wash me up. He told me to change my panties and gown. As soon as I was dressed, he told me if I ever told anybody what happened he would beat me himself and send me away from mama, my brothers, my sisters, and I would never see them again. He promised to watch me all the time to see if I told anyone. Then he told me to shut up and go to bed.

***

I remember that night as if it were now. It changed my life forever and took away my childhood. I was no longer the happy child that loved everything about life and glad to wake up and see a new day. That night, I became a woman trapped in a child's body.

The times that followed were always the same, always pain, always hurting! This happened two sometimes three times a week. When he wasn't fingering me while bathing or sleeping, he was penetrating me.

I know Mama saw the blood in my panties when she washed my clothes. Why didn't my mother care enough to question what was going on? How could she turn her head and not see what was going on in her daughter's life? Had this happened to her as a child and she didn't know what to do then as she didn't know what to do now? I hated being around him. I was scared when I would hear him come in the house. I remember wetting the bed or peeing on myself at six years old. I smiled and acted like it was okay, but deep inside I wanted to die. It only got worst with time and to add more fuel to the fire, I knew he was doing the same thing to my sisters. I may have been a child to the people on the outside, but I saw the change going on in my sisters. What could I do?

As I look back, I see the changes that took place in me, my sisters, and even mama. Mama changed from a grown woman to a submissive child obeying his commands. As I write, tears are streaming down my face. I dropped to my knees and cried uncontrollably. I asked God to strengthen me so I could complete my story and he restored me. When I laid down, I felt God's arms wrapped around me and I slept like a baby. When I woke up, I went back to the computer and started writing.

CHAPTER THREE

Why So Many Rules?

"For we do not wrestle against flesh and blood, but against the rulers, against the authorities, against the cosmic powers over this present darkness, against the spiritual forces of evil in the heavenly places."

Ephesians 6:12 English Standard Version (ESV)

Daddy took over 101 Parkview Place. Our dream home turned into a house of nightmares! He removed all the locks from the bedroom and bathroom doors. Since there were no locks on the bathroom door, he would push the door open and watch us. He convinced my mom he could help her wash us up while she did something else and she felt all right with it; but this gave him the opportunity to finger us and fondle us more. I was always scared. I cried all the time. When I went to the first grade, I would cry and wet on myself at school. When I got home from school, both would beat me for wetting my clothes.

Sometimes I even wondered why this was happening to me. I would see other girls in my class crying and thought they were scared because their Daddy was doing the same thing to them. I remember my first-grade graduation at school. He told Mama not to let me attend because I was such a bad girl. They made me stay home and I didn't go to school anymore that school year.

My life was so full of fear. You had so much to worry about. Just wondering if you were going to be with him that night or he was going to corner you somewhere doing the day. He had put a bed in the back room of the barbershop that he would call you to follow him back to. It would be so embarrassing out front with your sisters and brothers and they would see you leaving and know what was going to happen. My mom helped fix up the room in the back. As I remember he would get mad if you didn't move. You had to pretend you liked the act even though you didn't. This was one of the issues that I carried into my later life. I had to be reprogramed.

As the months turned into years, the molestation continued, but now it went even further. I was seven when he started to have oral sex with me. It was so disgusting. I hated him when he came in my mouth. I couldn't do anything about it, just do as he said or there would be trouble for me. At this point in my young life, I knew it was better to do whatever he said, and things wouldn't be so bad.

One night I walked into the bedroom that I shared with my other sisters and I saw my sister's legs in the air with Daddy on top of her. As I turned to run out the room, I heard her crying. As I looked back, I looked right into her eyes, I wanted to grab her from under him, but I was afraid. When I saw my sister the next morning, she looked at me sad. I couldn't help but think what was going through her mind, I wondered if she was mad at me for not helping her? We never ever talked about what was happening to us and what we saw.

He became so bold with his sexual encounters with me and my sisters that he would come into our bedroom at night. While all three of us, my two sisters and I, slept in the same bed, if he wanted to have sex with the one in the middle, he would not ask the other sisters to get up and leave out of the bed. He would just climb in and start having sex with anyone us while the other two laid still. Once he left the room, my sister would cry, and I would just hold her close until she went to sleep. I laid there and felt sorry for my sister. but deep down inside I felt guilty because in my mind I was glad it wasn't me. The next day deep in the back of my mind I was wondering if it were going to be me next.

As I got older, he stopped forcing himself on me as he did when I was a child. Daddy had this thing he always did to show more control. If he came to have sex with you and you started to cry or acted like you didn't want to be with him, he would just stop the act. He would go and tell Mama what happened. The next day he and my mom would beat me, and he would be fussing at my mom all day and she would run this guilt trip on me telling me,

"He's being mean to me because you are not doing what he wants. Why can't you be a good girl like everyone else?"

By the end of the day, I would be so tired of all the beatings and fussing. That night in order to get back in his good faith she instructed me to go to him and take off all my clothes and tell him I was sorry for the way I acted the night before. Then I had to ask him to have sex with me so that he could forgive me for the way I acted. Since I had given him a hard time, was so forceful that the following morning I was sore.

CHAPTER FOUR

The Stories He Told, The Changes He Made

"Love is patient, love is kind. It does not envy, it does not boast, it is not proud. ⁵ It does not dishonor others, it is not self-seeking, it is not easily angered, it keeps no record of wrongs. ⁶ Love does not delight in evil but rejoices with the truth. ⁷ It always protects, always trusts, always hopes, always perseveres."

1 Corinthians 13:4-7 New International Version (NIV)

He made more and more rules and restrictions for us to follow each day. First, we couldn't eat until he ate. Then we couldn't play with any outsiders. No neighborhood children were allowed in the yard. He even padlocked the front gate so no one could come in. We had to play with each other. It was alright sometimes playing with my sisters and brothers, but sometimes I would look out across the street and see other children playing and having a good time and I would wish I was one of them. We were not allowed to speak to them, if we were ever caught talking to them, we would be punished.

Another rule was when it was time to go to school, we were not allowed to ride the bus like my classmates. He took us to school. So, if school started at nine in the morning, then we arrived at eight fifty-five, just five minutes before school started. We would pull up in front of the school and jump out running to our classes so we would not be late. When school let out at three o'clock, we were to be outside by on time.

We couldn't participate any clubs or sports activities. He would visit the school at any time of the day, and I could have my head down doing my schoolwork, when I would look up, he would be standing in the classroom door, watching me. It made me so scared and very nervous trying to do my schoolwork and always checking to see if he was there. It made me feel vulnerable, knowing he was always there.

My life became even more confusing. I only went to school and back to the house. By the time I was 8yrs old, I became the mother for all my sisters and brothers. When I would leave school, I was responsible for all the cooking, cleaning, and washing. Mama put me in charge of my sisters and brothers because now they were coming to me for everything. I began to feel they were my own children, because they were my responsibility. My mom just read books and watched television all day.

She became pregnant again with another child by Daddy. She gave birth to another girl on a Friday the 13th, in August. They say this is an unlucky day, but this day brought joy as my beautiful sister was born. She was adorable, I loved her. Maybe it was more so I loved her innocence, or her little pain-free heart that was pumping blood through her little body. Whatever it was, I loved her, and I wanted to protect her from him. I wanted her to have the chance to be a little girl and grow up into womanhood, not the other way around like me and my sisters were experiencing.

After she was born, we were sent to my Aunt Peggy's house for a couple of days while Mama was in the hospital. Everyone was having a good time at Aunt Peggy and Uncle Harvey's house because while I was there, I didn't have to do the cooking, cleaning and taking care of my sisters and brothers. I could be a child for a while. I was looking at the television when the phone rang, and Daddy was calling to tell my aunt and uncle that he wanted us to come home. She started packing up our clothes and the doorbell rang. Daddy was at the door and when we left, they hugged us so tight. When I hugged my aunt, I began to cry softly so he would not see me.

When we arrived home my mom was there with my sister, Ashley Victoria Oakes. Mama was lying in bed and my work began. My brothers and sisters went outside and brought in wood for the pot-belly stove that sat in the middle of the room. They kept a hot fire going all through the night while I was in the kitchen making formula for the baby. I boiled the bottles and nipples and then boil the water for the Carnation milk and Karo syrup. I washed the diapers and hung them on a line behind the stove to dry.

Time was passing fast because I was working so much between home and school. The baby was growing fast, she was walking by the time she was nine months. She was a pretty little girl but sometimes it was hard dealing with all those children. I would go outdoors to hang the clothes on the line and would cry. I could not let Daddy or Mama see me cry because they would have thought I didn't want to do my duties and they would have given me a beating. As I would hang the clothes on the line, I would feel so sad, tired, and old wishing I was somewhere else. It was too much for me to handle. I would pray that God heard my prayers and would give me peace and comfort.

Mama started getting sick in the morning and throwing up all the time again. She told me she was having another baby. The baby, Ashley, was turning nineteen months when my mom had another girl named Aaliyah Renee Oakes. She was born on a Friday too.

One morning my mom got me and my brother up early to go to the commissary to buy groceries. She told me at the store that she may be going in the hospital to have the baby soon, so I was to get a turkey with all the trimmings, plenty of bread, potatoes, and roast, that way I could cook a big dinner for everybody. This would leave some extras for the next couple of days.

It was a hot day in June and after we came from the store, she went in the room to lie down while I started cleaning the turkey, washing the greens, and making the cake for dinner. My sister and I were washing clothes and hanging them out and bringing them in as they dried on the line. The fans were running, but they were only sending out hot air. As evening came, my mom said she was feeling bad. She started to cry loudly because her water broke. I ran into the room and my brother called 911, but the baby started coming out and the lady on the phone asked me how old I was. I said I was only nine years old, and she said I was old enough. Then she told me what to do. She told me how to hold the baby's head up until the baby was out. She wanted me to lay the baby on my mom's stomach after I wrapped her in a blanket. Then the doctors rushed in the house and they let me cut the cord. Then the ambulance took my mom away. Daddy came just as they were taking her away and he told us not to let anyone know Mama was gone from the house and that she had given birth to the baby.

He told me to finish cooking the dinner, feed the children, and then get them ready for bed and he said he would be by after work.

After I finished cooking, cleaning, feeding and putting everybody to bed, I was so tired I laid down with my sisters. I didn't hear him come in at all. I knew he was waking me up and putting me in my mom's bed so he could have sex. Once he finished, he told me he was leaving to go home to his wife and that I was not to open that door for anybody until he got back in the morning.

My aunt called the next morning asking to speak to my mom, so I told her she was gone to the store. She told me to tell her to call her when she got back. Daddy came in the morning, and I told him Aunt Peggy called. He asked me what I told her, and I told him I said

Mama was gone to the store. He said if she called again tell her the same thing. Around lunch time my aunt called back and asked for her. I told her again that she was gone to the store. She called late that evening and the next morning, and I continued to tell her the same thing. Early Wednesday morning she was knocking at the door. I was scared to open it because he had told me not to.

My Aunt Peggy became upset and told me to open the door at once or she was going to call the police. I did as she said and when she walked in, she asked where Mama was, Darnell told her she was at the hospital because she had the baby. She asked when she had the baby and Greg said she left Friday. My aunt asked who was keeping us and they all pointed at me. My aunt said for us to start packing our clothes because she was taking us home with her. Just as we were about to leave, Daddy pulled up in the yard. He jumped out the car and started fussing with my aunt, but she fussed right back at him, something I had never seen anyone else do. So, he finally let us all leave with her.

That evening while we were eating dinner and everybody was just laughing and enjoying Uncle Harvey telling jokes, the phone rang. My aunt answered the phone, and she was angry. She was telling my uncle that L.C. had wanted her to bring the children home right now because Mama was home from the hospital, but she told him the children had eaten and gone to bed. She said she knew it wasn't time for my mom to come home with the baby, but he was so mean he just wanted to prove his point that she was not supposed to take those children when he told them to stay.

The next morning when we got up, he was knocking and ringing the doorbell. My Aunt Peggy told us to get our clothes and she and Uncle Harvey bagged us some sandwiches and handed us each a bag. My Uncle Harvey was fussing at L.C. who became so mad he walked out and told us if we were not at the car when he got there, he would leave us.

We all rushed to get our clothes on and some of us were running to the car without our shoes on. He was cursing and fussing all the way home because we had let my aunt in the house. When he pulled in the yard and stopped the car, we all got out and ran in the house where Mama was in the bed holding the baby. I was glad to see her because it had been such a long time. But when Daddy came in the house, he was carrying a bunch of switches and he told us he was whipping us because we disobeyed his orders and opened the door while he was gone. He told us to line up and he beat the boys first. Then he beat the girls. He put these big welts on all of us, and some of the welt's marks cut so deep into our skin there was blood coming out. We were all crying and rubbing our arms and body from the whippings. He told us to shut up and get to work cleaning up and helping Mama with the baby.

My body was hurting and the welts on my leg and arm were bleeding. When he left to go back to the barber shop, my brothers and sisters came to me one by one so I could put some ointment on their arms and legs, and I held each one of them. I hurt because they hurt. I could feel the pain he had put on all of them and I cried softly.

Things continued as always until one morning just after he came in the house, there came this loud knocking on the front door and a woman was screaming his name.

"Luther, you bring your butt out of this woman's house! I heard she has had another baby by you. You come out now or I'm coming in!"

He was sitting at the table having a cup of coffee. He jumped up and ran out the back door and told my mom to lock the door. I looked out the front window and he was pulling her back in the street and putting her back in the car. Then he got into his car and they both drove away. This was not the last time she did this. The woman would come and fuss and fight with him. Daddy made it an order to always lock the doors if someone left out; if he found the doors unlocked, everybody would get a beating.

Another baby meant more work for us. Everything was an order or a rule. It was summer and school was out, but I never enjoyed it with all the responsibilities. My mom didn't help. She just made sure the work was done by me or my siblings. Cooking the meals sometimes was hard and keeping everybody straight so they would not get Daddy mad was hard. I felt I was responsible for all their mistakes.

When we finished the work at home, he would call for us to come to the barber shop. He would tell stories from the Bible. His favorite saying from the Bible was the story of this father who took his two daughters to the mountain and when they got there the two daughters got their Daddy drunk with wine and had sex with him. The two daughters became pregnant and God was so proud of this and He made their children holy and righteous. One day when he left the shop, I began to read the Bible so I could find that part of the story he always told us about. I became so amazed at what I was reading in the Bible, I did not hear him come in. He grabbed the Bible from me and asked what was I doing? I told him I was reading the Bible. He said I was never to touch the book again, and that he was to be the only one to read from it. I got a beating to set an example for the other children, and I never touched that book, the Bible, until I left home.

Another one of his favorite stories was this dirty story he told of when he was on the farm. He said he would go out in the field so he could play with his penis, masturbating. He said one time he had his pants down and there was a cow out in the field. The bull saw him and started to run toward him at great speed, so he jumped on the fence and the bull was coming closer, so he began to climb over it with his butt exposed and the cow started to lick his balls and He said,

"Gone cow,"

And the cow licked him again and he said,

"Gone cow."

He licked him again, he said,

"Gonne cow,"

And with that lick he came all over the fence.

He shared dirtier stories about how he took his fist and shoved it up the anus of a horse. He would hear the horse moan and he could feel they're cum on his hands and arm. He told these stories often and we would laugh at them to make him happy. That was our daily thing to do, make him happy and keep him happy by any means necessary.

The summer was long and full of work. I was glad for school so I could get a break from work at home. When I went back to school everyone was happy to see each other and they would talk about their summer and how they went on trips with their families, to the beaches and how they had such fun, but all I could say in my mind was I cooked and cleaned and took care of my sisters and brothers.

I even thought of how I was washing all day with the wringer washing machine. Daddy wouldn't let us change the rinse water all day because he considered it wasteful. To save even more, he told me when I finished washing the clothes, I was to bathe all the children in the rinse water and I better not change it. All the children would line up in the evening one by one to get in the tub and take a bath, first the girls and then the boys. We had to take our bath in that dirty water. This happened every wash day. When it was time to take baths in the house, we couldn't change the water. All the children used the same water.

Another rule was all the children had to stay out of school at least once a week to help around the house. The house had to be cleaned from top to bottom by the end of a school day. This also gave him a chance to leave the barber shop and come home and force himself on us. I would be in the house alone cleaning. My mom was always gone to the barbershop or out shopping. Sometimes I would be in the house cleaning so hard that I did not hear Daddy come in. All I knew was he was behind me, pulling my clothes up, and making me bend over the table or sofa. He would unzip his pants and push his penis inside of me. To block out this moment I would start singing a song in my head. I wanted to close out what was happening to me and most of the time by the time I had finished the song, he would be through.

His rule and regulations always benefited him. When I cooked the meals, he got the best. My mom always bought the whole chicken because he said it was cheaper to cut them up than to buy it by pieces. I was the one made to cut the chicken. I had to bag two bags of breasts and wings and two bags of legs and thighs which were for his use only. He counted the bags as I put them in the freezer. The only part the children could eat was the chicken's back. Every week he made us go from store to store buying packages of chicken backs. When I cooked, I had to fry his good pieces of chicken first. Then I could fry the backs for the children.

In the summer, when he would cut the watermelon he would sit and eat the heart of the melon and give us, the children, the rest. I remember one afternoon all of us were sitting on the back porch eating the leftover watermelon.

I said,

"When I grow up, I'm going to buy a lot of watermelons and put them under my bed and just eat all day until I get sick. The first part I am going to eat is the middle so I can see how it really tastes. I'm going to eat so much watermelon that I get sick."

Everybody laughed and laughed. Then as I turned around, there he was, standing in the door and mad at me. Daddy told me to go and get a switch and come inside. All the time I was pulling the leaves from the branch and walking in the house I was crying. He told me I was ungrateful and just a mean child. When he finished beating me, which seemed forever, my arms, legs, and back were burning, and I was crying so hard I couldn't catch my breath. Then he got in his car and left for the barber shop like he always did. When I went in the room, there was no one to hold me like I did my sisters and brothers after their beatings. Later that night my sister Tracy brought me some of her snack and ran fast out the room to keep from being caught.

Every day I realized how much more controlling he was. The fear he put in me that night when I was only five years old, set the stage for the rest of my life. Every day as the years passed by, I began to feel so dirty and no good. My body was nasty to me. Now when he would finish with his sex acts, I had to bathe. When I would start to wash my body and especially my vaginal area, I would scrub it so hard it would be raw, and I have the scars to show it now.

I cried to myself a lot and my heart hurt so much. I felt so all alone. Late at night after all the children were asleep and Daddy wasn't home from work, I would go to the open window and look out at the stars. I would dream I was this cute little girl who lived in this big house with no sisters and brothers, only me, Rose. In this big house little girls had a real daddy who would come to her tea parties with her dolls and was always happy. When this daddy came home from work, he would always bring her some type of toy. When he would come in and see her playing, he would laugh and smile. When he held her, it was to swing her high in the air until she got dizzy. When she would fall asleep on the floor, he would pick her up, carry her to bed, pull the covers on her, and kiss her good night. Her mother would let her play in her own room with her dolls and toys while she prepared dinner. Her mom just loved her because she was always hugging and kissing her. She would run the tub full of water with lots of bubbles and I was the only one who took a bath in that water. Then I heard the car pulling up in the yard and heard my mom jumping up off the sofa to open the door for him and my dream ended.

My mom made him a king, and we were told to address him as that sometimes. As the years passed and we girls got older, my mom began to teach us one by one in the art of bathing Daddy. After he had eaten his snack, he would get completely undressed and come lay down on the sofa. My mom would have two-foot tubs full of water, one with soapy water and the other clear water. She showed us how she wanted him to be bathed. She started with his face. She wanted the cloth to be soapy. We were to rub his face with the soapy water while he closed his eyes. After I had washed his face good, then I was to get the rinse cloth out of the clear water tub and wipe his face until all the suds were gone. Next, you had to wash and scrub his feet. After rinsing them and drying them in your lap, you had to lotion them down while you massaged each toe. Then you got up and changed the water in both tubs. When you brought the water back, he would be lying on top of the sheet completely naked and she showed me how to suds his whole body down and how to massage his penis. Then you would dry his body off and lotion him down. Then I had to kiss him on his mouth thanking him for the honor to have washed and bathed his body. If it were your night to bathe him, then it was your night to have sex with him. I learned to bathe him from head to toe just as early as I learned everything else.

Mama would be in the other room and know this was going on saying and doing nothing. I hated bathing him and I hated my mom for teaching me this, but what could my sisters or I do? I wish I was who I am now. Stop thinking in my mind and just speak out.

Sometimes in my mind because I couldn't speak out loud, I would be wondering about things that were happening, and why things were like they were, but then something would tell me, *"This is your mother and father, and they wouldn't tell me anything wrong. You are supposed to trust them because they are your parents."*

Sometimes I would pretend to be asleep when he came in because it seemed like this was my night, my turn to be with him. When I felt him waking me up, my heart would start to pound and beat harder. You could never say no to him. You just did it! To get me through his sexual acts I would say the Lord's Prayer or sing one of granddaddy's church songs at the cross, and when I had come to the end, he would be through.

It was hard listening to my sisters with him and when they would get back in the bed next to me crying, I would just hold them close and tight and comfort them until they went to sleep. I was never taught how to really love and be a good mother. I just did what a real mother does when her child is in pain. The next morning when I would see my sister, we would look each other in the face. There was never a word spoken between us, but the way we looked at each other was enough.

Sometimes when Daddy and Mama would punish them and send them to their rooms after beating them,

I would slip them food and tell them to hurry up and eat the food and watch them wipe their mouths so there would be nothing showing they had eaten anything. If they had been beaten, I would hug and hold them close but only a little while so I wouldn't get caught. I could see and feel that I was becoming their mom. When they would fight among themselves or fall and hurt themselves, they would call me to straighten the situation out or put a bandage on the sore. They never called mama or Daddy.

Daddy's thing was to embarrass us when we were bad. One day my brothers did something wrong, and he decided to beat them. He made them take off all their clothes and stand naked against the wall while he called everyone to come and watch him beat them. My brothers were so embarrassed, they took their hands and covered their private parts, and he began to beat them hard. During the beating they would hold their hands up, so their privates were exposed. Some of the children would laugh and this made them cry. He would send them to their room. When I looked at him, he had this smile on his face.

They were still crying and when I raised their shirts and looked at the welts all over them. I asked them to please stop crying as I put Vaseline all over their backs, legs, stomachs, faces, and even their private parts. I knew he wasn't going to feed them, so I sneaked them food before I started his dinner. The next day at dinner I gave them extra food to make them feel better.

When they became sick, I was the one who set the time to give their medicine. I took their temperatures and cleaned up after them if they threw up. When they coughed at night or whined for water, I was right there. My childhood was slipping away and my role as mother was becoming clearer.

My mom was not only aware of his constant abuse, but she encouraged it. I remember her saying to all the girls,

"Better to be an old man's sweetheart than a young man's fool."

I don't know how I made any good grades in school, yet I did, even with all I had to do. People at school thought I was the happiest person in the world because of my smile. But if the world only knew that every morning before I would leave out, I would look in the mirror and tell myself to smile. I would hold this fake smile all day and in the evening my face would be hurting. I did this throughout my life.

When I got to middle school, I wanted to sing in the chorus so bad I would daydream all the time. I would ask the teacher to be excused to the bathroom so I could walk by the chorus room and see them practicing in class. When the chorus would sing for a school program, I wished it was me on that stage singing in front of the classes.

Daddy and Mama's law was that there would be no extra activities at school if it wasn't during the school day. I could join the home economics class that taught you how to cook, clean, and sew. Sewing came in handy when it came time to hem his pants and sewing on buttons for his shirts. If I wanted anything new to wear, I had to make it myself from my allowance money that I earned. I was glad to make my own clothes because it gave me a chance to get something new to wear instead of more hand-me-downs. My sisters started using their money to buy material so I could make them new things, too.

While I was in middle school, I remember Daddy's mother, Mrs. Eva, had passed away and this was the first time I ever saw him cry. A few weeks after his mother passed, I overheard Daddy telling Mama that his Daddy, Grandpa Luther, was living all alone in Macon and he was sending his wife down there to clean his house, cook him a meal, and do whatever he wanted her to for him. He said his wife would go one week and she was to go the next week. My mama asked,

"Do I have to have sex with him?"

"Of course. You do whatever he wants you to do."

He began to tell her how it was all right for a wife to please her father–in-law. He said it was her duty to keep him from being lonely. My mom did as he said. While the boys were outside cutting and stacking the wood on the porch for his heater, she was inside pleasing Grandpa Luther. There became a change in my mom. She became quiet and more distant. I guess she felt like us now. She had no choice either. This went on for years. When we would go to Macon on Sunday to visit Grandpa Luther, I hated kissing him in the mouth, too. He would ask me to sit on his lap and he would always feel me. I was glad to hurry and get it over with so I could go on the porch.

Another rule was about the money he gave for allowance. If your allowance was three dollars and he gave it to you on Friday, by the next evening all the money had to be spent. You were not allowed to save any of this money. If he found you saving the money that he gave you for your allowance, he would beat you because he always wanted you to come to him for more money. He wanted you to depend on him for everything. If you saved money that would make you independent and let you know you could make it without him. It was his game of control. My sister Ashley thought she was outsmarting him by saving her money in a hole that was in the wall. She put all her spare change in the wall, not realizing you would have to tear the whole wall down to get it.

Daddy's way was always the right way. He had this sick obsession. He had this one fork he had to have at every meal. This fork was his and no one else could ever use it. One day I was so busy with dinner that I forgot to put 'his' fork out. He came in and sat down and began to eat and he screamed,

"This is not my fork!" and threw it to the floor.

I was so nervous. I brought in a hand full of forks and he looked at them one by one continuing to throw each one of them to the floor. My sisters kept bringing in more and he was fussing more until he found the right one. He called me in the room and showed me the right fork and said for me to remember this fork. Then he called the other children in too and showed them the fork. He said he wanted that fork each time he sat down to eat. So as soon as he finished eating and got up, one of us would grab that fork, wash that fork, and put that fork in a certain place in the cabinet; and when it was time for him to eat, we knew where to find his fork.

One day I was cooking dinner and setting his place at the table when I reached for "his" fork. I looked around and there was no one else there but me. I went into the kitchen and put some food on a plate. I took 'his' fork and started to eat with it, and for the first time I just laughed out loud because I was doing something, he did not want me to do and would never know. It felt good. When I looked in the room and saw him eating, I laughed again to myself. His food was always served before us. All the children would sit around like servants in the kitchen waiting for the master to finish eating his food.

My sister was like me, they wanted to wear new things to school too. So, I would make dresses, pants, blouses for them. If they bought the materials, I would make the articles for them.

Because my mom had the navy card to go to their thrift store that's where all our clothes came from. He would not let us shop in new stores. He was so cheap. And when I said he was cheap believe me. When it was time to return to school, he made us gather up all the clothes of all the children, wash them, and iron them. Then we had to see which clothes fitted which child. The week before Labor Day, my sisters and I would wash and iron all day. In the evening of Labor Day, I would wash the girls' hair, pressing and curling all their hair for school the next day. The only thing he would buy for back to school was a new pair of shoes, underwear, socks, notebook, and a book bag.

He would buy a large quantity of notebook paper and issue out only fifty sheets per week. If you ran out, then you had to borrow from someone in school or steal out of someone's notebook. When we went to school, he would buy a pack of pencils with erasers and cut the pencil into three parts. Every third time he issued them; you could get the part with the eraser.

If we drink tea with tea bag and it was six of us when we finished, we had to give it to him to hang on a line to reuse. He would buy two-ply bathroom tissue and we had to spin one-ply on an empty roll and another on another empty roll. He would get wood from houses that was torn down and made us pull the nails out and straighten them so they would be used again.

It was hard for me to keep my mind on my schoolwork as I got older. The girls were talking about parties their parents gave them, shopping, and mostly about boys. I feared boys. Even though I was in the eleventh grade, I had not held a conversation with one boy. When a boy tried to talk to me, I would walk away. I was afraid someone would tell Daddy they saw me talking to a boy and I would be punished.

In 1967 my brother, Darnell William Oakes Jr., was a senior in high school and I was entering my junior year. I remember being called to the office and my mother was there. In came my brother Darnell and she took us in a room and told us Darnell William Oakes, her husband, had died. I didn't know how to respond. I wanted to cry but how do you cry for someone you really did not know or never met? She took us home; I remember the phone kept ringing when Daddy came in. When the phone rang again, he told Mama not to answer it and he got loud.

"You are not going to Philadelphia or anywhere to bury Darnell Oakes! You can call them in Philadelphia and tell them they can just dump him in the river!"

I looked in my mother's eyes and I could see the hurt, this was the father of four of her children, but she had to do what he said. When the phone rang again that's what she said. She repeated the exact words to the person on the line. I later found out that my grandmother and aunts in Philadelphia went to the government and got help to bury him. My mom did not attend his funeral.

Years later I found out that when my sister left home, she wrote the veteran administration requesting Darnell Oakes, our daddy's papers from the Marines. The papers showed that my mom wrote the Marine Core inquiring about his benefits for her and her children thirty days after his death. She received a large lump sum of money, which she gave all to Luther Cornell Yates, Jr.

This was how Daddy began to acquire more properties in Wakefield County and all surrounding counties. He even bought real estate in his hometown of Macon, Virginia. He bought over twenty rental properties. L.C. loved bragging to his customers and people he met about his empire. He would sometimes lie about owning land in other states.

Daddy had some dogs that he let run free down the side of the house. We noticed that every night after he came in from work, he made it a part of his routine to go out and feed the dogs. Just moments after he was in the yard with the dogs, you would hear the dogs crying and whimpering. This would go on about twenty to thirty minutes each night. My sister and I would whisper to each other about why the dogs made so much noise.

That summer night of June 19th, 1969 was my sister Aaliyah's birthday. On the night of Aaliyah's birthday, we had cake and ice cream and sang *"Happy Birthday"* to her. When we finished serving everybody, they all ran to their beds because Daddy was going out to the dogs. Tracy and I had to wash the dishes and put them away because there were never supposed to be any dishes left in the sink at night. Then we heard the dogs and my sister said,

"Let's sneak out the door and see what is going on."

I said,

"No" because I was scared.

So, we went into our room and pressed our heads against the screen. As we looked out the window the moon was very bright. I pushed my head forward pushing the screen out farther and I saw what Daddy was doing. It shocked me until I could not move. He had his pants down and had his penis inside of the dog which was making the dog holler. I quickly pulled my head back and pulled my sister from the window before he saw us. We looked at each other and ran and jumped under the covers and never spoke of what we saw ever, and I mean ever.

Robert Alonzo Brown my biological father.

Ghonieteen DeBerry Brown my mother.

Pinrecko L. "P.L." Artise Jr. my stepfather

Tommy Arrington my beloved husband.

CHAPTER FIVE

I Just Wanted A Normal High School Year

"but those who hope in the Lord will renew their strength. They will soar on wings like eagles; they will run and not grow weary; they will walk and not be faint."

Isaiah 40:31 New International Version (NIV)

In the year of 1969, I was a senior in Riverview High School. Everyone was happy to be a senior, including me. I also had a sad feeling inside because this would be my last year in school. School was my only escape from the home on Parkview Place; but I tried to enjoy those last days.

When it came time to buy my class ring, I ran home and asked Mama for the money to buy one. She told me to ask Daddy for the ring.

When I went to ask him, I said,

"Daddy, this is my graduation and I know I try to do everything you ask me, and I do it well. But I saw this graduation ring with my birthstone, and I want this ring."

"Please, Daddy, please."

He told me to kiss him and I did, he put his tongue in my mouth which I hated but I had a goal in mind. Then he said he would buy it for me only if I went on a trip with him to Dover Downs for the weekend. I just gave him this weak smile and said,

"Who is going with us?"

He said,

"I will take Tracy."

Deep down inside I wanted to say no, but I knew if I came right out and just told him I did not want to go, then it would have been fussing and a beating from my mom because I had made him mad. So, I said yes, and this cat-like smile came across his face. He had won again.

That weekend we left for Dover Downs early Sunday morning. This was not the first time he had taken any of us girls out of town, but this was the first time for me. He drove all the way and we caught the ferry. We got out of the car and he took us on the top deck where a lot of people were standing. He made me hold his hand on one side and Tracy to hold his hand on the other side. He was feeling all over me like I was his wife on a honeymoon. I could see people looking at us like I was this young girl with an older man. When we got to Dover Downs, he got a hotel room. We got our stuff out of the car and went inside the hotel. When we passed the hotel desk clerk, Daddy told the man,

"Yes, we are going to enjoy this visit in your fair city and as soon as my wives and I clean up, we are going out to dinner".

I was so embarrassed. I looked back, and the man at the desk was whispering something to the other man that worked with him at the desk. I knew they were talking about us. When the man opened the door to our room carrying the bags in, I saw two beds. I had to laugh to myself because he was always so cheap, and this must have hurt his pocket to pay for two beds instead of one. My sister and I were slow at unpacking the clothes because we were waiting for Daddy to instruct us about the sleeping arrangements. Then he said,

"I will take this bed to the right and you gals can have the other bed."

I was happy Tracy, and I would be sleeping together. As we were laying out clean clothes so we could take a bath and go out to dinner, Tracy rushed into the bathroom because she saw a shower in the bathroom, and we did not have a shower at home. She was so excited to use one! This left Daddy and me in the room. He had gotten undressed and under the covers. He cleared his throat and told me to come and get in. I obeyed and while Tracy was in the shower, he was having sex with me. He came all over my legs. Tracy came out the bathroom. She just turned her head and got under the cover as I jumped up and ran into the bathroom to shower.

As I was showering, he came into the bathroom and climbed into the shower with me and made me bathe him from head to toe. I did not get to enjoy the shower at all. All I did was dry off and run and got into bed with my sister. Tracy was already asleep or pretending to be when he came out the shower. He said he was going to take a nap and then we were going out to dinner. My sister and I waited until we heard him snooze and tiptoed around the room getting dressed so when he woke, he would see us dressed and carry us to eat.

He finally woke up which was about two hours later. When he saw us dressed, he got up and dressed to go out. We went to this restaurant that served roast beef sandwiches. A man was cutting the beef right off the bone as it cooked. We walked the board walk until late and bought boxes of water taffy candy to carry home. When we got back to the hotel it was late, around twelve o'clock that Sunday night.

My sister and I both went into the bathroom together to change into our night clothes. When he went into the bathroom Tracy and I jumped under the cover and pretended to be asleep. But when he came out the bathroom, he was naked and walked around to the side of the bed and tapped Tracy on the shoulders to follow him. She got up and got into his bed. I could see the cover moving and him moaning. Then I peeked and saw Tracy run into the bathroom. As I waited for Tracy to come back and get into the bed with me, Daddy got up and tapped me on the shoulders. I was scared to move, and he tapped me again. I knew what he wanted, and I did not want to participate. What could I do but obey him? I got into his bed and there was a repeat of the sex act all over again. When he finished, I slowly got out the bed, and slowly went into the bathroom to wash up and then I got back into bed with my sister. When morning came, we were up and out of Dover Downs by nine.

We arrived home Monday evening, which meant me, and Tracy missed another school day. The next day I was told the deadline for the graduation ring deposit was due on the following day, which was Wednesday. When I got home from school that evening, I told Daddy that I needed the money for the ring the next day. He told me he wasn't going to buy the ring because I didn't need a graduation ring with all the rings he had put on my finger. I was hurt so bad I wanted to cry. Why did he lie to me to get me to go to Dover Downs? I really didn't have a choice.

He knew this would hurt me, but he was on this control thing. I said to myself I will not worry or act up about the ring because I wanted to go to the prom. There was this guy that asked me to go with him to the prom, Randolph Jenkins. He was good looking, and I felt so good that someone had the nerve to ask me.

My friends told me there were a lot of guys that wanted to talk to me, but they were afraid of Daddy. They heard things that went on inside our home. Some even said their mothers didn't want them to talk to me. I went home and asked my mom if I could go to the prom. Mama said I could ask Daddy when he came home for dinner. I cooked the best food that he liked and even made a cake. After serving him dinner I went into the dining room to ask if I could go to the prom. He looked around and pulled his glasses down on his nose and said,

"Who will you be going with?"

I said,

"Well, this boy asked me to the prom."

When I looked into his face, I saw this anger. He asked when I had time to stand around and talk to a boy.

I said,

"I did not stand around. He asked me when I was going to another class. He just walked with me fast to my next class and asked while we were walking."

Then that smile came on his face that I knew meant his answer would come with attachment.

He said, *"You can go to the prom if you want to."*

I was so happy I hugged him. Then he said he would have to escort me to the prom, and I said it would be all right because at least I would be going with a date. Then he said that he was my date. This meant he would be carrying me to the prom, and he was my date. I couldn't do anything but run to the bedroom and cry. What would I look like with my Daddy as my date? My mother came into the room and asked,

"Why are you crying? Its better he goes with you than some boy who would be feeling all over you by the end of the night. Either you take that choice or just not go."

I decided not to go at all. I didn't need any more people whispering and laughing at me.

This was my senior year. It was one of the worst years I ever experienced. When graduation night came, they asked us to be there one hour before we marched in. I arrived when everyone was already in line and I had to jump in. Everyone was laughing at me. I wanted to cry. After graduation ended, everyone was going to parties. When the graduation was over for me, I hugged my classmates, and Mama and Daddy were right there to take me home. I was home eating cake and ice cream on my graduation night with my family. That is all I got for the twelve years of school. I missed school because now my life was going to become being home or at the barbershop. I wanted to attend college but Daddy said "no". You can only go to barber's school and help him in his shop. I didn't want to be a barber. I still had no choice in deciding what I wanted to do with my life. Because I did not choose his way, I would be home twenty-four hours a day, seven days a week.

Then in March of 1971 his wife, Joann, died. On the day of the funeral, my mother dressed us all. Daddy came to the house before he left for the funeral to check us out and make sure he approved of the way we looked. When we arrived at the church, a lady directed us to sit in the back. Everyone seemed to turn around as we sat down. His oldest daughter screamed out that she didn't want us there. She was crying out for us to leave, but then Daddy made her quiet down. I wanted to get up and run out of the church, but the punishment would have been worse.

Within a week after his wife's funeral, he moved the three children to our house, Timothy, Bobby, and Gail. They had attitudes because they did not want to be at our house. I would hear Daddy and Mama talking about them. Then he called me in the room and said I was responsible for them. He said they were to obey me like I was their mother and if they gave me any trouble, I was to tell him. So, where there were two girls to a bed, I had to make it three girls to a bed. In the boys' room, we put a bunk bed to make more room for the two boys that had come to live with us.

They were scared because all their lives they knew about this woman their daddy had in Wakefield and they would hear their mother cussing and fussing about this other family. Now they had to live with us. It made more work for me, but during the weekends and the summer months, most of the children would go to the barbershop. This helped to keep the house clean even though there was more cooking and washing of clothes.

In 1971 Luther Cornell Yates Jr. had his name changed through the courts to Damien Cornell Yates. That was not all he changed, the closed in porch on Parkview Place was turned into his bedroom, Daddy's bedroom. Now that his wife was not there to go home to, he started staying at our house. For him to get to his bedroom, he had to pass through the girls' room.

So now things changed. We had to get out of bed and go in his bed in his bedroom. When he came to live with us, he bought this soap. To this day I hate the smell of it. It was Irish Spring soap. At night after he ate, he would be in the bathroom running water and washing up with that soap. Soon you would smell that Irish Spring soap coming out into the hallway. He would step out naked and head to his room touching one of the girls on her shoulder to follow him.

The sexual abuse continued, but now there was another girl in the house. One night I walked in the bedroom from washing dishes and there he was on top of Gail with her legs in the air. She was not like my sisters who cried, and I would hold them tightly afterwards. She was very cold and quiet and when I tried to comfort her, she just turned her back to me. I didn't know how to comfort her, and I could tell she was feeling sad and alone.

CHAPTER SIX

He Knew How to Begin it and How To End it

"¹ will love thee, O Lord, my strength. ² The Lord is my rock, and my fortress, and my deliverer; my God, my strength, in whom I will trust; my buckler, and the horn of my salvation, and my high tower."

Psalm 18:1-2 King James Version (KJV)

Daddy had this book he kept on the wall behind his barber chair. In the book was a calendar which held the due dates of all the girls' menstrual cycles. He knew when each of us began our cycles and he knew when they ended. This is how he began to get us pregnant. My sister Heather began to get sick, always throwing up. My mom made me take her to the Marine Hospital to see a doctor. I told the doctor I was nineteen when I was only sixteen. He told me she was pregnant. I rushed home to tell Mama that Heather was pregnant. She was only thirteen years old.

I overheard the conversation between mama and Daddy that night. My mom said to him that she was too young to have a baby and asked daddy what were they going to do? Within a week a lady came to the house, Ms. Victoria. She told my mom she needed a place to go with Heather. As she was waiting, mama told me to take her to the little apartment behind our house. It was a small apartment with a kitchen, bedroom, and bathroom.

Mama said she wanted me to help Ms. Victoria. I did not know what I was going to have to do. She told Heather to get undressed and put on this gown she handed to her. She told me to wash my hands. She opened a black bag that she had with her. When I came back into the room from washing my hands, she took out a long needle and a small needle. She put the small needle in Heather's arm. Then Heather started to get sleepy. Ms. Victoria cleaned her stomach with alcohol, and she pulled out this long needle which she put in Heather's navel. It contained a yellowish fluid. After she pulled it out, she told me to stay with Heather until she got back.

Hours passed before Heather woke up. She was crying because her stomach was hurting. She was crying hard. I ran to tell my mother she was hurting bad and she needed to call 911. She told me to go back with Heather. Then I heard Ms. Victoria coming in and she told me to wash my hands again because she needed me.

When I came back in the room, she had my sister's legs wide open and was telling her to push. I was holding Heather's hand when she told me to hand her a tool. Then she told me to hold the light so she could see. She told my sister to push harder. Next, I saw something I had never seen in my life. It looked like little baby birds with no skin, and they were very bloody. Now my sister was crying harder and louder and I was so scared I did not know what to do.

Ms. Victoria told me to run and get my mom and tell her to come right now. I was so scared I think I flew over to the house. Daddy and Mama were sitting at the table. I told them Ms. Victoria needed them to come right away, they jumped up and went over to the house. I was following close behind them. You could tell Ms. Victoria was upset. She said,

"Look at this, this girl just gave birth to twins."

She showed them this bloody white blanket. She opened the blanket up for Mama and daddy and they looked at the two bloody fetuses. Mama and Daddy just looked and did not say a word. However, Ms. Victoria had a lot to say.

"This is a child having a child and she is the youngest person I have ever performed an abortion on. God has to forgive me for what has happened here."

They said nothing and turned around and walked out the door. Heather was still crying. She did not understand what was happening to her. All she really knew was she was hurting, and she began to reach for me. I held her and cried with her. Ms. Victoria pointed at me and said,

"Go into the bathroom and get me a pail of warm water and some towels."

I moved as fast as I could. She told Heather to sit up as she placed the towels under her and washed and dried her off. Heather screamed again, I thought she was having another baby, but Ms. Victoria told her it was alright. Something did come out of her while the lady cleaned her up and I helped her put on a clean nightgown. Ms. Victoria gave her two pills as I handed her the water. Ms. Victoria thanked me for being such a good helper and left.

Heather was crying because she didn't like what happened to her. I told her to quiet down. I had to clean the mess she made. I helped Heather to a chair and gave her some soda while I changed the bed sheets. Once I finished changing the bed, I helped her into the bed and told her to watch television while I went to get soup for her. I gave her an aspirin with the soup and she finally fell asleep. This gave me time to cook dinner. I sent Tracy to check on her. When I finished cleaning the kitchen, I went back and stayed with her all night. She stayed in bed about three days.

Because he kept a record of our periods, month by month, which let him know our fertile times to conceive a child, this made us his prey, this meant he could get anyone of us pregnant at any time he wanted us to be pregnant. That was not the only abortion Ms. Victoria did for him. She performed abortions on all the girls, Tracy, Aaliyah, Gail, and Ashley. She did one more abortion on Heather at the house. Then she did one at her house with me helping her there. She told Daddy and Mama she was not going to do anymore abortions on Heather. She did two abortions on Ashley at the apartment and one at her house too. At her house in Stony Green, she had this room set up like a doctor's examination room, cold and sterile, with white cabinets on the wall full of bottles, gauze and white towels staked high on the counter. There was a rolling chair and a big light. The floor had white tile and was shiny, but it was cold in the room. I believe he got us all pregnant because he could plan it by our dates of our periods but most importantly to him was controlling when he could get us pregnant.

My sister Tracy was tall and loved having a lot of hair that flowed in the wind. Daddy would always hurt her feelings by calling her "Bubble eyes" because she had big eyes, but her eyes were what made her beautiful. She had a natural mole on her face like the movie stars. She and I were close. She was only one year younger than I, so she saw everything like I did. Tracy had an outgoing personality, but her feelings were easy to hurt. She was not the one who helped with the cooking, but she would clean the house with me. Also, she could do a good job in keeping the children quiet and putting them to sleep. She tried so hard to please Daddy, but when he wanted to be mean he knew how to make her cry by calling her "Bubble eyes." He started laughing loud which made the children join in, and my sister would just cry and cry. Daddy had taken so much from her too. She was very insecure with how beautiful she was. Yes, she was a beautiful, dark skinned girl with a lot going for her, but Daddy had this way of making the whole family feel that slavery mentality that the bright skinned persons were better than the dark ones. Because Tracy and I were so close, we knew how to get around some of his games. She learned like I did that if you did not want to be beaten all day, you just submit to him that night. If you made him laugh at something you did or you just hugged him for nothing, then sometimes he would overlook you that night and go with someone else. Tracy was always good at playing sick. We used to always call her a good actress. If she knew he was coming to her on Wednesday, then she would start having pains in her side on Sunday. She couldn't get up and even move out of bed by that Wednesday so that was not her night. This went on for a while until he caught on. Then came the day Tracy got pregnant, but when she found out, Daddy and Mama tried to make her keep the baby.

Mama fussed so much making Tracy feel guilty, but she held her grounds and said no. She did not want a baby. They called Ms. Victoria and as we drove to her house, Mama fussed all the way there. The years had taken a toll on her too, affecting her mind and will. After Ashley had the ability to get up and leave, that was always on Tracy's mind. Tracy and I always talked of leaving, and we started planning her escape.

I had this best friend, Kaleen Young who knew what was going on. She and I would talk on the phone when Mama and Daddy would be at the shop. When I told her, I wanted to help get Tracy away and out of the house, she said she would help. We knew she would need clothes because he was not about to let anyone leave with anything but the clothes their back. This is how he treated the older ones when they left.

Kaleen told us that we could bring clothes to her house, and once we were out, we could come and get them. Tracy knew she did not have any family to go to, so when she was supposed to go to the doctor, I dropped her off at the Army recruiter so she could join the Army. We had decided that at least if she was in the Army, she would have a place to stay. They would feed her, and she could make some money. Tracy did not need my mom or Daddy to sign anything, once she signed the papers, she was set to go. Tracy had talked with my Aunt Peggy, my mother's sister, about the plan. She told Tracy she wanted her to come to her house and she would help her. So that night while Tracy was supposed to be driving me to the barber shop, she went to my Aunt Peggy's house. We spoke with Kaleen and she knew if my mom came by and questioned her, she knew nothing. At least Tracy had a change of clothes. I felt all right with her at Aunt Peggy's house. Tracy was free!

The whole house was in an uproar for weeks after this happened. I was questioned day and night because Daddy said I had to have known she was planning to leave. My allowance was taken away for weeks and he treated me meaner, but at least I helped my sister. Another one of my children was out of this evil place!

Years later I visited Ms. Victoria's house. I looked her address up in the white pages and called her. The phone rang three times before someone answered. The person on the other end was Ms. Victoria's daughter. I introduced myself as Rose and I explained to her some of the reasons I needed to speak with Ms. Victoria. She told me her mother had passed about six months before. I asked her if I could come out to talk with her and she said yes. I drove to her house with thoughts the first time I was in the car with my sister Heather and mama driving. I knew we were going to Ms. Victoria's house because I heard Mama and Daddy talking about the plan. I knew Heather was pregnant again, and he wanted this pregnancy to be terminated. After all my sisters had abortions that were ordered by him, I saw, and I watched each one of their lives changed. I saw the hurt and I could feel their pain as the years took their childhood away. I wanted to hate my mom and dad, but they took that away from me too. I did not know how to hate, I did not know how to love, and I did not even know how to be angry.

As mama, Heather, and I pulled in front of Ms. Victoria's house, I reached over and held Heather's hand. She was always very cold and distracted from things that went on around her. She wanted my hugs and caring ways, but on the surface, she tried to show the hard-outer side of being cold. Daddy had taken that away from her too. Deep down Heather was caring and loving, but he had beaten her so much for rebelling against his sexual advantages that she hid that part from everyone. I knew it hurt every time she had abortions, not the physical pain but the mental pain. I knew it hurt, but he did not care. He never considered our souls or our hearts or questioned why or how we felt. It was always about him. It was about pleasing him no matter how bad we felt. Even though we became pregnant and had him growing inside of us, still, we had no choice. Then after the abortion, life was still the same until another one of us became pregnant.

I began to think of the other times I had gone with my other sisters. As I pulled into the driveway of Ms. Victoria's house, tears consumed me. I cried like a baby. I composed myself and got out the car to ring the doorbell. Ms. Victoria's daughter answered and invited me in. We sat down and talked for over an hour I asked if I could see the room. The room was still set up the same as I first saw it when I carried my sisters there. In my mind I could see her working on my sisters and a cold chill ran over my body. Then came the uncontrollable tears. I cried like the times they cried when she had finished her work. I felt like fainting, but I turned and ran. The woman stood in the door as I got into the car. I never went there again.

I remember once after Ashley had her abortion; Daddy came into the room. I had placed her in a gown and told her to lie down. He was so mean to her. He looked at her lying there, weak and helpless, and all he could say was,

"Did you think you were going to keep this baby? Remember I gave it to you, and I can take it away. You are a bad girl, and you deserve no joy because you don't please me. Maybe one day you will please me the way I want you to and see that I am the one you need to obey."

He was so cold to her and this made her cold. My sister Ashley was a pretty girl. When I say pretty, I mean like a movie star. Her skin was smooth and clear. She had a nice shape and a smile that could win an Oscar. She looked just like him. She talked like him and even sometimes laughed like him, Damien Cornell Yates. She looked like he spit her out of his mouth, like the old folks used to say.

As the years went on, you could see Ashley hated that she looked like him. Ashley was my hero. She fought him every chance she could, and she did not back down. When she had something to say, she would say it even when he would beat her. Sometimes she would get two to three beatings a day, but she got to the point she stopped showing him tears. You could see he was beating her more so she could cry but she was so stubborn she held back those tears. I was crying out loud for her and pleading with him to stop.

"Daddy please stop, please stop beating her. She is sorry, Ashley tells him you are sorry, please."

She saw me crying and spoke softly,

"I am sorry."

Then he stopped.

One day when Ashley was thirteen, she left school with this boy named Phillip Hines. That was one of Daddy's days to visit the school unannounced, and he found out Ashley was not in school. When she arrived home that evening, Mama beat her unmercifully. When she finished beating on her there was huge and open welts all over her body. Then mama called Daddy; when he got there, he went outside to get his own switches. When he came back in; he started beating on Ashley too. His blows were harder and longer. Ashley fell to the floor and balled up into a ball as he continued to swing. All the children were begging him to stop. My mom watched and did nothing to stop him. This time he beat her so long Ashley was crying and pleading for him to stop. Being she was light skinned, the bruises were dark and bloody.

When he left for the shop, he put her in the room and ordered that nobody was to feed her or go in there; but when I got the chance, my sister Tracy guarded the door while I sneaked in. There she was in a corner crying. I pulled her clothes back and saw the welts all over her. I hugged her and I cried with her. She looked tired and lost and all I could do was hold her close and try to ease her pain. Even though I was in that room for only a few minutes, it felt like time stood still. Then and only then did I question God.

I was crying out,

"Why Lord? Why is this happening? Tell me what to do. I don't know what to do or what to say to make her feel better."

Then that little girl left my mind and body, and the adult came out and told me to first help her heal the wounds on the outside. Then try to heal the hurt inside. As the days went on, I learned to help heal her inside pain a little. That was the hardest time in my life when I did not know what to do to help my children.

That same night he came into the room and had sex with her. A couple of days later mama went to the school and told them Ashley was moving to South Carolina with her brother and wouldn't be going to school there anymore. She told this lie so Daddy could get more control of her. He took her out of school at the age of fourteen. This gave him the whole day to molest her and break her will. Through all the beatings and bad treatment and with mama agreeing to all those abortions back-to-back, Ashley still remained strong the best she could. On the night of her eighteenth birthday at twelve o'clock, she walked out that house and never came back again. I was so happy for her and I prayed she never had to return to that house again. Every time he got any of my sisters pregnant, you could see the pleasure in his eyes of the power he had gained. He loved the control. He loved the way he could control so many lost souls. The more power he gained, the more he used his power as control.

He started letting my brothers, Darnell and Greg, have girlfriends. When the girls would come around to see my brothers, I would tell the girls to leave because this was not the place you wanted to be. I tried to tell them about Daddy, but they saw the money and flashy cars and they did not listen to me. He let Darnell's girlfriend move into the small apartment in the yard that was used by Ms. Victoria to do abortions. The girl my brother was dating was only thirteen years old and he was twenty-two. During the day when Darnell would go to work, Daddy would go to the house, and I knew what he was doing. In a few months she was pregnant and when the baby was born it looked just like him. My brother knew what this man was doing to his girlfriend, but he seemed to only want to please

Daddy. If sleeping with his girl pleased Daddy, and then it was all right.

My other brother Greg met a girl and he tried to do the same to her, but she did not go for it. She had a big family, and they knew the way he was. Her brothers came to Daddy and told him they would kill him if he ever touched her. My brother married her and moved out on his own.

In the meantime, my brother Darnell's girlfriend got pregnant again and again. One day I was sitting out in the yard and she started crying and telling me how Daddy was coming over every day while Darnell was gone. She did not want to have sex with him, but he made her, and she did not know what to do. What could I tell her? All I said was to go back home. Then she started crying saying she now had three children and was only sixteen years old. I told her to tell my brother what he was doing to her and she said, holding her head down,

"Your brother said it was all right for him to share me with his father."

CHAPTER SEVEN

Daddy Will Be So Proud

"5 Trust in the Lord with all thine heart; and lean not unto thine own understanding. 6 In all thy ways acknowledge him, and he shall direct thy paths. 7 Be not wise in thine own eyes: fear the Lord, and depart from evil."

Proverbs 3:4-6 King James Version (KJV)

I prayed and prayed to never get pregnant. Then, on March 9, 1973, it happened to me. My whole world just rocked on its foundation. I went to the clinic that morning because I was having pains in my stomach. They ran these tests, and the doctor came in and said I was pregnant. I started to cry and when it hit me what he was saying, I cried louder and louder. I started to plead with the nurses and doctor telling them,

"Please, I cannot have this baby. You don't understand. I cannot have this baby."

I was shouting so loudly they had the nurse give me some medicine. They couldn't shut me up. They called Mama to come over there. After they told her why I was upset she came in the room. She was not upset like I thought she would be. She walked into the doctor's office with this smile on her face. All she could say was,

"Daddy is going to be so happy. You can get whatever you want. I hope it's a boy and he look like him."

I cried all the way to the barber shop, and when I got out of the car and ran to the back room crying. Mama ran to Daddy and told him the good news. He ran to me and started feeling my stomach. She told him I was four and a half months pregnant. Then she said to him,

"You were not wrong about the date at all."

Then it really hit me. He knew I was pregnant the whole time and so did my mother. I was nineteen years old, and now he had done what he had been doing to my sisters, planning all our pregnancies. I just lost it and ran into the middle of 17th Street and just laid there. I was hoping someone driving by would not see me lying in the street and just run over me. My mom and my sister ran out to pull me back into the shop. Throughout the evening until I fell asleep, I cried. When I woke up during the night and remembered what was happening, I wanted to kill myself. I wished I could have gotten an abortion, but the doctor said I was too far gone. I did not want to have this baby. I wanted to die. Mama and Daddy was so happy and did not care about how I felt.

Every day I carried this baby I felt bad because I felt everyone in town knew it was by Daddy. If people did not know I was carrying his child, he would make sure they knew. Now I felt even worse. You could always see that sneaky smile after he let them know. If he could belittle you in anyway, he made sure he did not miss the opportunity. On August 19, 1973 on a Sunday at noon, I had the baby. It was a boy. He was very light skinned, and he looked just like him. That evening all my sisters and brothers came over to the hospital and when I walked down the hall to the nursery, I looked in the glass and there he was. I wanted to name my son Brandon. I loved that name, but when my mom heard me say that she came back that night and fussed and fussed. She told me I had no right to pick a name, that the baby was his, and he had the right to pick the name. Why do you want to make him mad? She was so intimidating that I named him after him, Damien Cornell Yates Jr. When I brought my son home, I did not want to touch him. I did not want to look at him because I knew whose baby it was, and I was not happy. My sisters took care of my baby for me. I would pray every night to be showed the love I needed to give my baby, then one day I said to myself,

"My baby is a part of me too and he needs me."

I stepped in and started loving him. I loved my baby because he was so handsome. I did not have the thoughts of him looking like Daddy; God hid that away from my eyes and from that day on he looked like me. I loved him then as I do now.

I told daddy there was not enough room for me and my baby in the one bedroom that I shared with my other sisters. He had an apartment next door to the house, which he let me, and my baby move into. It was nice just being out of that house and it was fun buying things for my house. I felt really grown up but that did not last long. About two nights after I had moved in and was fast asleep, I was woken up to him climbing in my bed. It made me feel worse because now I was afraid to go to sleep. I am so tired of this life. I wish I was dead.

All the customers that came into the shop knew this was his child, and he began to tell everyone I was his wife. Some people would look at him amazed by what he was saying. I guess they couldn't understand how he was so bold. Then he would say he was a Muslim and he had seven wives. They were Tracy, Ashley, Heather, Mama, Gail, Aaliyah, and me, Rose.

That summer my Aunt Isabella, who we called Aunt Bell, was having a family reunion at her house in Forestville, N.C. and sent us an invitation. All my mother's brothers and sisters came down. Cousins were there from New York, Ohio, California, and all over North Carolina. I was happy he was letting us go, but I knew Daddy wasn't going to buy the children any new clothes to wear to the reunion, so I made outfits for all the children to wear. I went to the secondhand store to get outfits for my brothers to wear. My mother went to the store and bought a new store outfit. That morning the boys cleaned the van and car for the trip to my aunt's house. It was good hitting the road going anywhere beside home.

When we got there, we all had to sit together at one table. We sat there the whole time. If one of us got up and talked to our cousins, he would send one of the children to tell us to come and sit down at the table with him.

If anyone wanted to talk to us, he would stop what he was saying and listen to our conversation. D.C. made sure they all knew Damien Cornell Yates Jr. was his baby. I was so embarrassed. Some of my cousins were very friendly. One of my cousins bent over and whispered in my ear that she was here for me and if I ever wanted to leave just call her. She said she hated him. He stood up and was headed my way, my cousin stood up and acted as if she was talking about the baby. After she left, he asked me what she was telling me. I told him she was asking the size of my baby's clothes because she wanted to get him a gift before she went back home.

When it was time for the food to be served, I heard everyone talking about how my mom fixed him the first plate. My Aunt Bell was serving the children first, then the older people, and everyone else followed. But as soon as she saw the food being served, my mom jumped up and grabbed the first plate and made Daddy's food first and then gave him the plate. Everyone was whispering how she made sure he was fed first like he was a king. Everybody could see how much control he had on this family.

Then there were people there who wanted to hear him talk about his new religion, so he did. He told them how he could have as many wives as he wanted, and the Muslims allowed it. He told how it was all right for him to be with his daughters and how Mama was the head madam in his tribe. I was glad when we left. I prayed that we would never have to attend a reunion with him again. I know God heard that prayer because that was the last reunion I ever went to with Mama and Daddy. When I went to another reunion I had moved out and was on my own.

After the reunion some of my aunts came to my mother's house because she was having a small cookout. My Aunt Mae and Uncle George were there with two of their granddaughters. When Daddy came out on the porch, he complimented the girls on how pretty they were. All the evening he was right on them telling them if they spent the rest of the summer with us, he would buy them all their school clothes and pay their way back to Maryland.

My Aunt Mae was excited about the offer. She was telling them it was all right and making plans to pick them up in two weeks. I knew what he was planning to do to them, so I went to my aunt to tell her to please not leave them here because something was going to happen to the girls. She told me not to worry because Maureen would not let anything happen to her grandchildren. She wouldn't listen to me. My aunt and uncle packed their things up and left for home. It was about eight that night before they hit the road.

That night I cleaned up and left for my house next door. I was up late cleaning my kitchen when I heard someone screaming. It was one of the girls. She had run out the house and was running around the house to my grandmother's house, which was around the corner. In a little while my grandmother came back without her. I came through the back door and the other little girl who was twelve was crying in the kitchen. I heard my grandmother fussing at my mom as to why she let him do that to those girls. She told Mama to dress the other girl and she left out the house with her.

The next morning my Aunt Peggy was right there coming into the yard and the way she was walking, I knew she was mad. I went to the back door and heard her fussing at D.C. about what she heard. She said she was there for the girls' clothes and she was screaming at Mama. Just then, the phone rang but they were fussing so loudly they did not hear it. I went inside to answer the phone. It was my cousin, Candice. She wanted to speak to my mom. I went to tell her that Candice was on the phone. Then D.C. came into the room and my Aunt Peggy jumped on him. I was going to hang the phone up, but my cousin was so upset. She was crying and fussing and cussing at the same time. She said,

"Aunt Maureen, how could you let him have sex with my girls? I trusted you, but I am catching the next plane out of here and I am bringing some of my Rastafarian friends and they are going to hurt your husband."

D.C. got on the line and told her those girls were liars and this never happened. She hung the phone up. He left that day and was gone for almost a week. My cousin did come down that same day and took her girls back. She was very angry and was crying with every word that came out her mouth.

"All these years I have protected my children then I send them down here to my Auntie and she let this happen to them".

I could tell she was hurt. This man just had no regards for anyone, whether it was family or not. My cousin never spoke to him again. But years later, after I had left home, she and I talked at length about my situation and how she was still hurting. She took that hurt with her to her grave. I felt so sorry for her.

CHAPTER EIGHT

Why Did You Bring Me Back?

"Now the Lord is the Spirit, and where the Spirit of the Lord is, there is freedom."

2 Corinthians 3:17 English Standard Version (ESV)

That winter Daddy was having lots of problems with his car and he found this mechanic that had a garage. He would get me to drop the car off and someone would pick me up. There was this guy that worked there, Carlton Wayne. He was cute, had long hair that he wore in a ponytail, and he was light skinned. Sometimes I would sit and talk with him for about thirty minutes before I would call and have someone pick me up.

One month there was a show at the Omni Mirage in Sheridan, a city in North Carolina about 15 miles from Wakefield. It was an Earth, Wind, & Fire show, and he said he would take me; however, I told him about my Daddy. He said he understood. We decided to meet each other there. Daddy agreed that Tracy, Heather, and I could go, but all of us were meeting someone at the show. It was nice to finally be out with someone. Carlton was the first in my nineteen years. I wished it could last longer but the time seemed to move faster than ever. Because we all went our separate ways, we made a meeting place after the show.

We started walking and went downstairs at the Omni Mirage and there was an elevator. We got on the elevator and started to kiss. He told me how much he liked me and wanted me to be his girl. Then one thing led to another and there I was having sex with Carlton in a stopped elevator. We started to rush back to the show to see Earth, Wind, & Fire, but I looked at Carlton differently. This was the first time in my nineteen years I had ever been with a boy other than Daddy. This was the first time another man told me he loved me. This was the first time a man ever held me like he really cared about me.

I began to tell him about my Daddy and the things he was doing and how I wanted to get away from there. He listened to me every time I could sneak a call to his auto shop and talk. Then one day he said.

"I get paid next Friday and if you can find an apartment, we can move in together."

This sounded like the best thing for me. At least I would be leaving Mama, Daddy, all that work, and that home with all that hurt and pain. Within two weeks I found an apartment with one bedroom, kitchen, a nice yard, and a living room. That evening when Damien, my son, came home, I took the last of our clothes to the house and called Carlton to pick me up around the corner. When I walked into my apartment, I felt free for once in my life. Carlton brought food for me to cook but sometimes he brought in cooked food. I stayed in most of the time. We would ride out late at night and he would tell me how Daddy would come by the shop every day and ask had they seen me. He acted as if he didn't know where I was.

After about three weeks, I noticed when he would tell me about how my Daddy and brothers were questioning him about me, it seemed different. He started talking about how hard it was paying this bill and that bill and how much my parents could help us more. Then one day he came in and said he had talked to my parents. He told me they said they would let me come back and that he could come and live with me. He said they would help us. I cried all night because I did not want to go, but if he went with me, I thought I would be safe. We moved in one of the apartments on the yard known as the "Compound."

My mom and Daddy did not seem mad at me but seemed to be glad I was back; it was just a front. Carlton started working for Daddy. He would pay him and for a while it was working in my favor.

Then in the mornings when Carlton left for work with my brother, Daddy would come over to my house saying he wanted to have coffee. One morning while I lay in the bed asleep, I heard the door open; it was him wearing only his robe. He told me Carlton said it was all right. I was so scared I started to cry, and he said with this smile on his face, that smile that let me know he had won again,

"I had to pay him a lot to get you back home."

This sent a sharp pain through my heart because I now had found out Carlton's reason for insisting that I go back home. I laid there with no emotions, no feeling. I felt completely hollow. When he left, I went to bathe. I scrubbed my body so hard and long that my body became wrinkled. I was crying so hard the time just passed.

When Carlton walked in the house that night, I met him at the door and smacked his face so hard it hurt my hand. I was screaming and crying at the same time. Now I did not know what to do. I told him what had happened, and he did not say a word. So, this meant I had to start secretly saving all the money I could to get away. Then I found out I was pregnant again. I became depressed and every time Daddy came and had sex with me, I wanted to kill myself. When he found out I was pregnant, he would tell me it was his child, not Carlton's. This made carrying this child just like my first child because I did not want another baby by him. When this baby was born it was light skinned but the baby had a lot of Carlton's features. I was glad; deep down inside I knew it belonged to Carlton; however, whenever Daddy was alone with me, he said this was his child because he had planned the pregnancy.

Things were harder to do because now I was sleeping with these two traitors and I wasn't saving as fast as I wanted to. One day Daddy bought Carlton a car, the kind he always wanted. He started coming in later and later and then one day he said he was moving out. I asked if he was taking me with him. He responded no and said that my Daddy would take care of me. I did not want to stay there, and he knew it. My sister Heather came and told me that she had heard that Daddy had given Carlton a car and some money to leave me so it must have been true.

When I heard this, I wanted to kill myself. I stopped eating, stopped caring, and when I was alone, I was thinking of ways I could end my life. One morning I walked into Butler Clinical Hospital in Sheridan. When they asked me what my problem was, I told the lady I was tired, and I wanted to kill myself. The lady rushed me into the back and then doctors came in and asked a lot of questions. I told them about the things my Daddy did to my sisters and me. They moved me to the mental ward of the hospital, and I was put to sleep. It seemed like I slept for a week. Several doctors came in and talked with me. At some point my mother came in and started telling me I had better get it together and come out of this hospital. I wanted to stay because I felt safe and they were helping me.

The social worker told me because I was over eighteen, I had the right to check myself in and check myself out. My mother had no control over that. A police lady came in to talk to me. She said I could take Daddy to court for what he was doing. I told her I was too frightened, because he might harm me and my children. I started to cry, because I knew he was already angry because I would not check myself out.

I had been in the hospital over six months before I was strong and had some direction in my life. The day I was being released, a social worker came in and said she could help me get some food stamps and a check for the children. When my mom and Daddy came to pick me up from the hospital, I told them about the different medicines I was on. I said I was going to move out to my own apartment with my two boys and the child I was now carrying.

Then my mom went into her pity lecture on how I needed to come back home so she could help me take care of the children and take care of me. They took me back to the apartment in the yard and I started to pack my things and began to look for an apartment. My mom left me packing and the very next morning she was right there at my door. She said Daddy understood that I wanted my own apartment; he said he would rent me the house he had in Wakefield. This way she could help me with the kids during the day. If this was all right with me, she would have my brothers' start moving my things. I asked if this was going to be my place that Daddy or nobody else would have a key. I also asked her if this meant Daddy would come to my house when he wanted to.

She said,

I agreed I would move there. When I got back to the
house, they started moving my things to Wakefield.
My brother Greg was assigned to help me move, he
had some of his friends to help. He was going with this
girl named Shelia. They lived on the other side of town
and she brought her brother, Orlando Madison to help.
It took all day to move my things. Once we finished,
my brother brought in a bottle of Southern Comfort
and we sent out for food. We all just sat around and
laughed, it felt good being with other people. We
unpacked and hung pictures until late. I put the
children to bed, told everyone goodnight, and went to
bed.

The next morning when I woke up, I was in pain; I
went to the hospital where I gave birth to this beautiful
little girl, whom I named Alexis. When I looked at her
face, I knew she could never be alone with Daddy. At
that moment I promised the Lord I would protect her
for the rest of my life. My brother, Shelia, and Orlando
were over almost every day helping with the children
and getting me settled in. It wasn't anything Orlando

would not do for my sons. Once he asked Damien what kind of candy he liked, and he told him he wanted some life savers candy.

When he came back that night and walked into the door, he did not bring one pack of life savers, he brought this bag with every flavor of life saver there was. I couldn't do anything but laugh. I was laughing more, and things seemed to be alright. I sent all the children to bed and we talked.

He asked me about my Daddy and listened to me for hours about this man. He heard about him and wanted to know if he was going to come in whenever he wanted to and would there be some trouble. I said no because this was my place, and he had no key. But in the back of my mind, I was thinking about how Daddy kept asking me for a key to my apartment and I kept saying,

"No. This is my apartment and I do not want to give my key out."

We listened to music and talked. He told me he liked me, and deep down inside I had begun to like him too. He was different. He was easy to talk to. He seemed to be so caring. He had no children, was not seeing anyone, and I liked being in his presence. By now we had known each other for about a month and a half. It was around two in the morning and I told him

I had to get up and dress the boys for school and go to the shop. We kissed each other good night and he left.

Once I was in the bed, the phone rang. It was Orlando. He said he was at his sister's house, we talked all night, when I looked out the window the sun was rising, it was dawn. I rushed to shower and woke the children for breakfast. I dressed the children. I grabbed their schoolbooks and I got them into the car for school. However, there was something wrong with the car. Daddy had Darnell go get the man to come out and fix the car while someone dropped me off at the barber shop. I called Orlando and spoke with him until I saw mama and Daddy pull up in front of the shop. Daddy said the car would be finished by two. When the car was brought to me, I picked up the boys and we all went home so I could fix dinner. Orlando called about six and asked if he could come over. I said yes but it would have to be around nine thirty because I had to help them with their homework and bathe them and get their clothes ready for school the next day.

A knock came on the door at exactly nine thirty. He came into the kitchen and watched me clean the kitchen and he even dried the dishes. I checked on the children's room and they were all asleep. They were at peace.

I invited him upstairs to my room. He was so gentle as he kissed me, and he slowly undressed me. It felt different this time. He kissed me the whole time and rubbed my body, making me feel special. This was the third man I had sex with in my twenty-six years of life. He made me feel like somebody, a woman. Then he held me close and he did not just jump up and run out the room. He held me close to him in his arms and he made me feel for the first time in my life so alive. As the music was playing on the stereo, I just fell off to sleep, believing in my mind this was the fantasy I had dreamed of.

Then, as I was sleeping peacefully, I heard someone putting a key in my door and pushing on it as it opened. I jumped straight up. This scared me because I was the only one with the two keys. Orlando said,

"Who is that? Don't worry. I have my gun."

He jumped to the floor and got his gun just as I heard a voice. It was my Daddy, and he was hollering for me to come and open this door. I started to shake and told Orlando that was my dad and to stay quietly in the room. I grabbed my robe and started down the steps. He was pushing on the door trying to break the chain that held the door closed. I said,

"All right, I'm coming."

As I reached the bottom of the steps I said,

"What are you doing here and how did you get my key?"

He said,

"When your car broke down today, I had a duplicate key made so I could come and check on you. I had been asking for a key for over a month and who told you to put a chain on this door?"

I removed the chain, and he came in. I said,

"I don't need you to come in and check on me."

He said,

"Why? Is there someone here?"

I said,

"It is none of your business who I have in my apartment. This is my apartment, and I pay rent here."

Just as I finished talking, things got quiet. Then I heard movement upstairs and so did he. He pushed passed me and headed up the stairs. I saw the gun he had pulled out of his pocket.

I screamed,

"Orlando, he has a gun!"

Daddy said,

"He better come on down here before I shoot him."

Orlando said

"I am not scared of you and you are not going to shoot me because I have a gun myself."

So now it was a standoff. Orlando turned on the light in the hallway and stepped out. When Daddy saw who it was, he said

"Oh, you are Shelia's brother. What are you doing here with my wife? You better get the hell out of here."

Orlando came down the stairs backing him back down. He said,

"Man, you are sick, messing with your beautiful daughters like you do."

Daddy was at the bottom of the steps and was putting his gun to the side. Orlando stood up to him and would not back down like everyone else. He looked at me still holding the gun in sight, and said,

"Rose are you alright? Mister Yates you had better not put your hands on her, or I will deal with you myself."

He reached for the door and whispered,

"I am here for you".

Then he left.

Daddy was mad. He wanted to hit me, but he didn't. He was calling me a whore and a bitch and a good for nothing, and then he started pulling the phone out the wall. He was screaming and so was I telling him to leave my house. There was a knock on the door, and when he answered it there stood two Wakefield Police Officers. He asked what they wanted. They said they wanted to talk to the lady of the house. I stepped out from behind him as Daddy said to the police

"Everything is alright you can leave."

They told him to step out on the porch. One stood outside and the other came in to speak with me. I was crying so hard he told me to sit down. My boys ran to be with me. The officer said we know who Mr. Yates is and we have been to this address on several occasions. I explained that this was my apartment and I rented from him. He was on the porch telling the police officer he wanted me out the house now. I became more upset and the police officer that was in the house with me asked if I had a lease or receipt to prove this was my apartment. I went to the drawer and showed him the lease and receipt. He told me everything was going to be alright.

The officer went on the porch and asked him if the children and I could stay until tomorrow because it was so late. D.C. said,

"No, I want them out on the street right now."

The officer said,

"Mr. Yates, I just wanted to see if you were like I had heard. Why would you want to put your daughter out on the streets this late in the night with nowhere for her and her children to go? The lease does say she is renting this apartment from you, but you will have to go through the court to have her evicted and you will have to show a good cause."

The other police officer said,

"Mr. Yates you will have to leave and give her key back because she has proof this is her apartment and I can take her down police headquarters to take out a peace warrant on you, so I advise you to leave and leave now."

He handed the key to the officer and left. They told me to lock the door and they would be out there to make sure he did not return. I thanked them and I put the children back in their beds and watched them fall to sleep. I was so upset and depressed again. I cut off the bright light and headed upstairs.

As I reached the top and walked into my bedroom I began to cry. I cried and cried, then I opened the drawer near my bed, and I saw the gun. This was a gun I kept by my bed because I lived alone. Suddenly, it hit me. My life was never going to get any better. There was no happiness for me in this lifetime. I have tried and tried. There is no one whom I can trust. I thought I could trust my mom and she gave me to the wolves. I thought I could trust Carlton and he sold me to the wolf. I have no friends and no family that will help me. I have three children. One child I know by my Daddy. I have this little girl and I refuse to let him have her like my mom let him have me. I love my children. He is never going to leave me alone. Not ever. God I cannot take this anymore. I am tired of fighting.

I looked at the gun. I rubbed the gun. I checked to see if there were bullets in the chamber and there were six bullets. Then after checking the gun to see if it was loaded, I sat on the bed and put the gun in my mouth and silently asked God to please forgive me. As I put my hand to the trigger, something said you don't want to leave your children here with him and your mother to raise. I slowly took the gun out of my mouth and I decided I had to take all my kids with me. I will not let their life be like the life I am leaving. I got up and started slowly down the stairs. I was making plans on which child I would shoot first. I considered shooting my oldest son first, then Brandon, my second son, and last my daughter, the baby. I could then shoot myself knowing I was not leaving my children behind. I prayed God would forgive me. This is the right and only thing to do. I reached the bottom step. I took a deep breath, wiped the tears and made a step into my children room. As I reached for the light switch, there was a knock at my door. I was so into the mind frame of carrying out my plan I almost did not hear the voice asking me to open the door. I suddenly stopped. And then there was a knock. I put the gun to my side and asked who it was.

"This is Orlando, open the door. C'mon Rose please open the door"!

I said

"What?"

"This is Orlando, please open the door".

I opened the door for him. He asked if everything was alright then he looked in my hand and saw the gun. He took it from me and asked what I was doing with this gun. I started to tell him of my plan and how close I was to carrying it out. He said he called the police and watched until they left. He was glad he came back. He said this is not the way you should deal with this. I told him to leave and let me do what I needed to do. I told him I didn't want to be like my mother.

Then he said,

"No, I cannot leave you and these children. What can I do?"

I looked at him and said

"Just take me away. If you help me and my children get away, I will owe you."

And he did take us away. It was turning dawn and he said he would help me. I gathered all my children in his car and left. We left with only the clothes on our back. The next evening Orlando and I went back to my apartment to pack my things, but to my surprise everything was gone. The house was empty. They had taken everything. I called mama and I asked her who moved my things. She said if I come back home then I can have everything back, When I told her I was never coming back she said I would never get anything back. I told her I needed clothes for the children. I said just once can't you get me a suitcase of clothes for your grandchildren, not for me. I will meet you somewhere and get them. She said she wasn't going to do that for me, and I hung up the phone.

I did not really know this man. I learned about him only after I left with him. He was a good man. He found us an apartment in Sheridan, and he began to raise all three of these children as his. When my nerves where bad and my crying was uncontrollable, he took the kids out and played with them or took them to the movies so I could have quiet times to myself.

He got a job working in a restaurant. He worked hard to provide for me and my children, He said he wanted me to be home with the children, but I told him I wanted to help. I said I would work part time, and this was alright with him if I was happy. Working part time gave me time for the children after school. I did the cooking, washing clothes and just keeping the house clean. I was feeling so good about my new life.

Then one day I walked to the store to get something for dinner, and as I was returning from the store when I saw Daddy's car parked down the street. He was in it. I ran quickly around the apartment building and into my back door. My heart was pounding so hard I began to cry. I made sure the doors were locked and called Orlando at work. He told me to calm down, stop crying and to stay in the house. He came right home and drove up next to his car. I could see him pointing his finger. Orlando was getting louder, and I was dialing the police, when I saw D.C. pull off.

Orlando came into the house and he just held me. He told me D.C. would not be back and he was getting me a gun for protection. I asked Orlando what Daddy said. D.C. told him to send his wife back home and Orlando told him he was a sick puppy. Orlando told him he better not be seen in this area anymore. Daddy said he had a right to be on city streets. Orlando said Daddy got the massage and left. He said he had something for him if he bothered me again. He told me to drop him off at work and don't walk by myself anymore.

The next morning when I got back from dropping Orlando off to work there was an envelope inside the door with no name or address. I went to the phone to call Orlando and he told me to bring it to him. When I got to his job, he opened the envelope and there was a tape inside. He put it in the car tape player, and it said this is for my wife Rose and the song he wanted me to play was, "She Used to Be My Girl". Orlando was mad. He asked for the day off. We drove to Lambton to a gun shop. He bought a 357magnum. I asked what he was going to do.

He said,

"Let him know I mean what I say."

We went back to the house and there was Daddy sitting in front of the house. Orlando told me to go into the house and he walked to dad's car. When I looked out the window, I saw him and Orlando coming to the door. When he sat down, Orlando pulled the gun out and laid it on the table. He told him that if he ever caught him sitting in front of his house again, he was going to use that gun. Daddy stood up and left and from that day on we never saw him again. Orlando was an angel sent by God. Three years later he married me. Our three children were in our wedding. My sister and I had a double wedding on May 18th. The invitation we sent to mama and daddy was sent back to us burned in an envelope. I was given away by Orlando's uncle; my mama's brother gave my sister away. Daddy told his family not to attend our wedding and they did not come. But GOD had a beautiful day for us. We had a good time and I never thought of them that day.

***

This story you have just read is about a controlling man, who caused so much hurt and pain to so many people for many years. This man had no heart and when you look deeper, he had no soul. He never cared about the damage he inflicted on the young or the old. His game was for his satisfaction. I did look back. And the years that followed from my childhood until I left there at twenty-six years old was nothing but pain. Once I was on my own with three children, I realized I could not get through all those thoughts in my head alone.

I needed professional help. It has been over fifty psychiatrists and different medications the last twenty-five years. The hardest and the most painful question I asked every doctor I went to was, *"Why my mom never loved me?"* I just want her to tell me that she loved me because through all my childhood I cannot remember my mom ever calling me to her and just hugging me close or saying she loved me. That little girl wanted that hug then and that little girl wants that hug now. To this very day I still ask if my mom ever loved me.

I pray every day and every night and almost every hour. When I wake up in the morning and open my eyes, I say my prayers thanking God for being in my life. Because through it all He was there. When I look back, I realize when I was a child God was there because he saw my mind was too weak to handle all the abuse my Daddy and mother was putting on me. He closed that part of my mind and kept it safe with him until I was matured enough to handle all that pain and all that hurt.

I feel writing this book has freed my soul of the past. Writing this book has been not only painful but healing. I looked back into my past, opening that door that was always closing and opening on its own. I found that little girl that I lost at the age of five. I talked to her and I got to hug her and let her be a part of my present. For the first time in my life, I am living in the present and I feel great. I want everyone who has read this book to know you can be a savior, because God is the only one who can bring you through.

You see, it was like this story I heard long ago. This story is about a man that made pottery. He would take a piece of clay in his hands and sometimes it would take him hours just to make a perfect piece of pottery. But one day he got a piece of clay and started on his new project, but something was wrong with the clay. The piece of clay would not bend when he wanted it to bend, it would not hold together when he needed it to be firm, so he broke it into pieces right in the potter's floor. This man decided to throw those pieces of clay away. Man will throw away broken pieces, but God is not like man, He loves to work with the broken pieces.

You see I was those broken pieces. I was not broken in half but in many pieces. There was only one person who did not throw me away. It was GOD that took my broken pieces in his hands and saw what nobody else saw. He saw that I needed his grace and his mercy to form a new mold. My master took this old clay and pulled out all the hatred, all the pain, all the hurt and he put on a new layer of skin, took all that old childhood stuff away by teaching me spiritual love, faith, and patience. When I went down in that water for my baptism, HE washed it all away. All my sins were washed away in his sight. I was a new Rose. I found the real spiritual side of me. HE gave me the greatest gift of all, the gift of forgiveness through Jesus Christ. Our only hope of salvation is through the Son of the living God. Forgiveness makes me able to deal with my past so I can face the future.

I had to humble myself and ask God to show me how to forgive the people whom I trusted the most, my Daddy and my mother. I went to him on his sick bed and told him I forgave him for what he had done to me all those years and when I walked out that hospital room that Sunday night, I felt like the weight of the world was off me. He died the next evening.

I went to visit my mom and I noticed a change had taken place in my life where my husband and I were baptized, and I wanted to share this great feeling and journey with my mother. I told her how good I felt. I told her how I knew that God was there all the while. I was so happy. I hoped she was happy for me. When I went to kiss Mama goodbye and tell her I was leaving, I bent down close to her face.

She whispered to me, I raised my head and looked at her. All I could say was

"Mama, I love you and I can say I have forgiven you for not being there for me. I am sorry you are still in denial, but I cannot deal with this anymore."

I walked out and asked God to help me because when I got into the car, I was so full of tears. She hurt me again. I want to let everyone that reads this book know that God was in the midst of all of the abuse this man imposed on everyone who came across his path, but God was always there because he promised to never leave us. I asked GOD to show me the right path. I am so glad for all the faith I have in God.

Without Him I am lost. I need Him every day and I need him for everything in my life.

TO GOD BE THE GLORY.

Which road do I choose? The mature family tree begins at its roots. Generations after generations of families are what make the tree stand tall and make the leaves and branches full and strong. A family tree begins with the first generation of a mother and father, and to this union a child.

The guideline to making a child become the second generation is the pathway their parent's show them. Their childhood should be filled with their mother's and father's love. Because of the great trust and love a child has in their parents, they will do as they are told because young children would never feel as if their parents would intentionally try to hurt them. There are some occasions when the dependency that children have toward their parents, is used in a negative way against them.

The hugs and kisses the child receives help build their character for love. Giving helps with the humanity. Being obedient is for strength to help them to endure. A mother and father are responsible for teaching a child all their positives and negatives in life. The child looks to his parents for all the guidance and understanding for his life.

When I decided to write this book, it was not written out of hate, or revenge or to even cause any more pain to my family. This was one of the hardest decisions I had to make in my life. After all those years I discovered I had not healed. I prayed, and I prayed, and I prayed, every day, all day long. I prayed about it so long that the hours turned into days, and the days into weeks and the weeks turned into months which turned into years. While this book sat on the shelf, I tried to go on with my life.

I laughed when my heart was hurting. To the people on the street, I looked like I had the world on a silver platter. I was smiling when my life was way out of control. I wanted desperately to move on with my life and release all that pain from my past.

One day my husband, Orlando, told me something he had heard his co-worker say. He said, *"You cannot move forward until you let go of that past."* He didn't know what he was asking of me. He wanted me to go into that past. I thought he was out of his mind, what he wanted me to do was indeed out the question.

When I looked back, I could see all of those years that were full of hurt, frustration, and unforgiveness. There were times I just didn't want to live. Being there in that past only would bring up so much shame, low self-esteem, and no hope in sight. What I would find was a home without true love. There were scars all over my arms, legs, and body. There also were spiritual scars that were not visible to the eyes, the ones that were deep down beneath my skin on the inside. If my husband loved me the way he said he did he would not have asked me to return behind those gates of hell.

Orlando promised me he would be there for me and walk every step with me thru the good and the bad until death separated us. He kept his promise and walked with me on this journey for twenty-five years. He left me and went home with God in 2004.

After his passing, I would go to the ocean and listen to the waves because I could always feel God's presence there. It was always peaceful there. I could sit and cry to Him, I would find myself talking and reflecting on all the issues my husband dealt with. My husband would see me crying morning, noon, and night and I would scream after waking up to a dark bedroom with my heart racing and pounding like it
was about to explode.

There always was this constant feeling of terror and always jumping out of my skin when my husband was only reaching out to comfort me. I was a ball of nerves. He and I talked about the nightmares and how I would just shake all over when he would reach to cuddle me. I was such a light sleeper I barely slept the whole night. I did that because I was so afraid of being asleep when "Daddy" would come into my room and molest me, I just wanted to be awake when he touched me.

After my children had gone to sleep Orlando and I would talk for hours and when I talked enough, I would start to cry, that's when he would just hold me close in his arms until I fell asleep. I felt safe. I felt loved. I missed him then and I miss him now. Now that he is gone, who will I talk to? Who can I trust with all my secrets?

My children were my inspiration not to give up hope because a better day would come. When I looked at them it helped me realize that God was always there. I look at my children, so innocent, so full of life, so trusting, looking at me to guide them on the right path of life and having to show them right from wrong. The important message from God was to protect His children, which He has blessed us with. Needleless to say, my past hurt my children too. They tried to understand why I was so depressed and cried so much. I was so protective of them. I didn't let them spend the night over anyone's house.

At family parties, or any gatherings I was always watching my children, seeing where they were all the time. I was so overprotective and always asking questions on the personal level. I would rather have ten kids in my back yard then to let my children go play in their friend's yard.

How could my mom have not been there to protect us from that monster? She knew and helped him with his devilish ways. Why didn't she take us away from him? Why didn't she have the mother instinct to not let this happen to us? Where was the love? I not only show my children I love them; I tell them I loved them every chance I get.

When I would go for therapy, which I attended for over twenty –five years, the first question I asked was, "Why didn't my mom love me? Throughout my whole life I can remember a lot of things, but I cannot ever remember my mom saying she loved me, or remembering her just holding me close, or taking up for me. He made her turn so cold and unlovable which turned her away from her own children. Was your love so strong for him that you could turn your back and choose not to see what he was doing to us? The man known as *"Daddy"* all my life was a cold hearted, controlling, and manipulative person. How could she let that man rob all of us of our innocence, our childhood, our life?

The road she took was the road that led to deceit and pain on her children for the rest of their life. I knew what I had to do, and it was to face those demons that were sucking my life out of me. Even though this happened decades ago, that first tear I cried when I was that little girl of five was the tears I cry today as an adult. I realized that I was stuck, I could not move forward. I needed to find out why mama or "Daddy" was like that. I believe this happened to them too, but their hurt was so bad they felt it was alright to cause this terrible, horrifying pain to me and my siblings. They had a choice like everyone else in this world. I realized I had to make a choice in my life for me, my children, my husband. I had to first find the spiritual healing, that meant getting closer to God. This meant I had to forgive them.

To someone who has never forgiven someone, it may look very easy for them to confess they forgive you. But to truly mean it and allow it to set you free is a difficult task. You are being asked to face the person in your life who hurt you so bad. You know what, I did forgive them. I am here to tell you it can be done, but only with God's help.

This book was written to help someone who is going thru this or experienced this in their past. I hope my testimony of God's grace, kindness, and mercy will change anyone who picks this book up to read. I just want to tell them that I am a survivor and to let them know there is nothing impossible for God. I love everyone. I love this life God has given me. I thought I would never feel that part of me, now that little girl has been set free. Thank you, LORD!

About the Author

Rose Arrington joined the Hampton Roads Ventures Board in August of 2012. Rose has been an advocate for improving her community for many years. This appointment provides her with another opportunity to fulfill her mission to champion economic self-sufficiency for socially and economically challenged families, particularly those in public housing.

She has served on the Board of Directors of several non-profit agencies, whose missions benefited economically and socially disadvantaged populations, including Community Housing Services, The Center for Community and Family Services, The He Ain't Heavy Foundation and Northwest Manors Affordable Housing Development Corporation. She currently serves on the Board of Directors for the Legal Aid Society of Eastern Virginia. She has managed polling venues and coordinated voter registration events.

Rose is also an advocate for creating opportunities for grief counseling within the public housing community. She believes that grief counseling is a staple missing from these communities, particularly since these families experience tragedy, per capita, at a much higher rate than families in other communities. She knows first-hand experiencing the tragic loss of both her teen-aged son, followed several years later by the tragic loss of her husband due to social and economic disadvantage. These tragedies have provided her with a passion and special insight that makes her a better champion for her cause. She is an advocate for Victims of Violent Crimes, Victims of Domestic Violence and Victims of Child Abuse.

Rose is a member of the First Baptist Church of Lamberts Point in Norfolk, Virginia.

Real Characters

Rose..Rose Marie Arrington
Orlando...Tommy Arrington
Alexis...Anonymous
Damien Cornell Yates Jr.................................Pinrecko Artis
Channing...Jason Lloyd Artis
Jada...Shaniya Artis
Maureen Oakes.............Mother Dear/Ghonieteen Brown
Luther Cornell Yates, Jr................Pinrecko Lloyd Artis Jr.
(Name changed in 1971 from Percy Lloyd Artis Jr.)
Darnell Williams Oakes................Robert Alonzo Brown
Darnell W. Oakes Jr...................................... Anonymous
Greg T. Oakes... Anonymous
Tracey V. Oakes......................................Anonymous
Ruby Wright... Anonymous
Walley Wright..…. Anonymous
Aaliyah Renee Oakes......................................Anonymous
Eva and Luther Yates Sr........................... Anonymous
Heather Annette Oakes............................ Anonymous
Gordan..…… Anonymous
Joanne Reid Yates......................................Anonymous
Aunt Peggy.. Anonymous
Uncle Harvey.. Anonymous
Ashley Victoria Oakes.............................. Anonymous
Randolph Jenkins......................................… Anonymous
Timothy...…… Anonymous
Bobby.. Anonymous
Gail... Anonymous
Ms. Victoria.. Anonymous

Message From The Author:
Rose Arrington

I first have to give glory and honor to God! It is because of Jesus Christ I am here today to share my testimony, and encourage other survivors of child sexual abuse that God is with us. His word says He will never leave us nor forsake us, and it is only because of God that I can share my victory.

To my husband, Tommy Arrington, of twenty-five years, I give my heart, love, and thanks for always being in my life. He was a good person with a good heart and caring soul. When he walked into my life it was a mess. He saved my three children and me. Tommy never complained. He just raised and loved Pinrecko, Jayson, Rosemarie from the first day he met me. After three years he asked me to marry him. He made a vow to me that he would never leave me and would always be there to walk every step with me, thru all the good and bad until death separate us. On January 4, 2004 he passed away in my arms early that Monday morning. I am so glad I was there when he took his last breath to go home with the Father. Thank you, God for sending a man like him into my life. I call your name every day and I "miss you so much baby".

To my three children, Pinrecko Lloyd Artis my oldest son, Jayson Lloyd Artis my middle son, Rosemarie A. Artis-Freeman my only girl, you were my inspiration to keep fighting to survivor. Yes, they were on this journey that consumed my life with pain and sadness, and I look at their lives and it consumed them to. They were there when I was trying to get some order in my life. I am so sorry to have touched each and every one of their lives with my past. I love all my children to the moon and back. On August 4, 1998 Jayson Lloyd Artis was murdered in Tijuana Mexico by the police after the FBI investigation.

I want to give honor and thanks to a man who sent support and provided for his four children and three that belonged to my mother's 'boyfriend. My family told me how much he loved us even though he was not able to see us. His name is Robert Alonzo Brown Sr. a Navy officer. Rest in heaven Daddy.

To my sisters and brothers that shared this horrible childhood with me. I love you. We always have each other, no matter what may come our way. There is a bond between us that Daddy could not break, could not take away. And while we didn't have the traditional upbringing, that has not hindered our love for one another.

To all my family and friends, those who have shown support in various ways I thank you! Words only cannot measure the appreciation that I have for you who have helped me, listened to me, and allowed me to share my truth!

Last but not least, I would like to thank my SH Publishing brothers, Darnell Basnight and Clifton Johnson. These are my brothers in Christ, and they have stepped in and been more than just publishers. They are my family. We have shared many conversations, tears, joys, and laughter, and I know that I can always count on both of you to have my back. I love you both.

When I am not advocating for the rights of survivors of child sexual abuse, I work at the Hampton Roads Ventures Board since August of 2012. I am passionate about improving the community. This opportunity provides me with another opportunity to fulfill my mission to champion economic self-sufficiency for socially and economically challenged families, particularly those in public housing.

I have served on the Board of Directors of several non-profit agencies, whose missions benefited economically and socially disadvantaged populations, including Community Housing Services, The Center for Community and Family Services, The He Ain't Heavy Foundation and Northwest Manors Affordable Housing Development Corporation. I currently serve on the Board of Directors for the Legal Aid Society of Eastern Virginia. I have also managed polling venues & coordinated voter registration events.

My focus is on creating opportunities for grief counseling within the public housing community. I believe that grief counseling is a staple missing from these communities, particularly since these families experience tragedy, per capita, at a much higher rate than families in other communities. I know first-hand experiencing the tragic loss of my teen-aged son, followed several years later by the tragic loss of my husband due to social and economic disadvantage. These tragedies have provided me with a passion and special insight that makes me a better champion for these causes. I remain an advocate for Victims of Violent Crimes, Victims of Domestic Violence and Victims of Child Abuse.

7-Day Journal: One Day at a Time

DAY ONE

This was a long and very painful journey. Holding on to God's hand and finding the spiritual part of yourself is the beginning .

Going to the beach even in the winter when it cold, just listening to the waves roaring in and rolling out. Such a warm and loving feeling. It lets me know I am in his presence. Just give it all to Him.

Where can you go to be alone with God, to talk and tell Him about your hurt and pain?

Psalm 18:2

"The LORD is my rock and my fortress and my deliverer, my God, my rock, in whom I take refuge, my shield, and the horn of my salvation, my stronghold."

DAY TWO

Take time for yourself. I love going to the nail shop, or shopping by myself. I feel good doing things on my own because I never had that freedom. Because we have gotten in the way of always helping others, how will you begin taking time for yourself?

Matthew 11:28-30
"Come to me, all who labor and are heavy laden, and I will give you rest. Take my yoke upon you, and learn from me, for I am gentle and lowly in heart, and you will find rest for your souls. For my yoke is easy, and my burden is light."

DAY THREE

Peace. Finding the peace in your life is a struggle. You have to move on from that past which I found in psychiatrist and medicine for the depression . Many years of talking and even now. Please always pray. How do you find peace in your life?

Philippians 4:6-7
"Do not be anxious about anything, but in every situation, by prayer and petition, with thanksgiving, present your requests to God. And the peace of God, which transcends all understanding, will guard your hearts and your minds in Christ Jesus."

DAY FOUR

The greatest part of this journey was learning to forgive, not going to the abusers per say, but forgiveness for yourself. This is so you can move on and not get stuck. How are you going to forgive yourself? How are you going to forgive those that hurt you?

1 Ephesians 4:32
"Be kind and compassionate to one another, forgiving each other, just as in Christ God forgave you."

DAY FIVE

Congratulations, you made it to Day #5. It wasn't easy, and there may be rough days ahead of you, but right now, in this very moment, you are surviving. It's always about taking One Day at a time. Some of us may need one hour, minutes, even seconds. Go at your pace, a pace that is safe for you but challenges you to be your truth!

Psalm 59:16

"16 But I will sing of your strength, in the morning I will sing of your love; for you are my fortress, my refuge in times of trouble."

DAY SIX

The Bible says God made man and woman on the sixth day. God created you too, on a special day for a special person. You are not what you have been through. You are alive, you are special, you are unconditionally loved by God. The sexual abuse tried to destroy you, but it didn't. You are a survivor, survive!

Jeremiah 29:11
"For I know the plans I have for you", declares the Lord, "plans to prosper you and not harm you, plans to give you hope and a future."

DAY SEVEN

Day Seven atlas, breathe in...breathe out...! Yes the journey continues, repeat the days as many times as you like. Start your own routine to keep you focused and moving forward. It may never get easy, but you will get stronger. This is the moment you realize that God has been with you through it all, and He will comfort you.

John 16:33

"I have told you these things, so that in me you may have peace. In this world you will have trouble. But take heart! I have overcome the world."

<u>Were You There?</u>

Were You there when I came into this world? A beautiful baby, with a head full of curls.

Were You there when He came into my bed that night? That's when he took my innocence and spoiled my life. Were You there when I cried and cried because I hurt, and did You hear my prayers, and how I doubted it even worked?

Were You there when I hugged my siblings who cried out for love? Just like how I pulled them so close like a mama tiger does cubs.

Were You there when I said enough is enough? When I walked from that hell and said no more stuff!

Yes, You were there thru it all, You helped me to be strong, and stand tall.

When I said tomorrow, You let me thru that door with all my sorrows.

With peace and love, You held my hands. You carried me like the footprints in the sand.

You were my Mother, my Father, my Everything, You held me thru that storm and rain.

Were You there, I don't wonder anymore. Because I am here and not on the other side of the door.

Written by: Rose Arrington

The Consummate Flower

A precious seed planted in soil that may have been tainted with lies,

Yet my roots dug deeper into the ground so that my soul could rise.

My stem is standing strong, with the promises of a different forever,

Trouble don't last always, and I know through God it well get better.

Through my trials and tribulations, my spirit was being cultivated,

There were times in the cold of winter I thought I would not make it.

It was God, who brought me patience to handle the situations,

And at the appointed time, I was made free from a lifetime of frustrations.

My blossoms in the moments of spring, reminded me of the beauty in me,

For my salvation was uplifted to perfection because
Christ loved me.

A sowed flower in the kingdom of God for the entire
world to see.

By: Cliff "Vizhun" Johnson

Psalms 23

The LORD Is My Shepherd

A Psalm of David.

1 The LORD is my shepherd; I shall not want.

2 He maketh me to lie down in green pastures: he leadeth me beside the still waters.

3 He restoreth my soul: he leadeth me in the paths of righteousness for his name's sake.

4 Yea, though I walk through the valley of the shadow of death, I will fear no evil: for thou art with me; thy rod and thy staff they comfort me.

5 Thou preparest a table before me in the presence of mine enemies: thou anointest my head with oil; my cup runneth over.

6 Surely goodness and mercy shall follow me all the days of my life: and I will dwell in the house of the LORD forever.

If you know something, say something!

National Center for Missing & Exploited Children's CyberTipline

Call 1-800-843-5678
Call 24 hours everyday

National Sexual Assault Telephone Hotline | RAINNwww.rainn.org

When you call 800.656.HOPE (4673), you'll to be routed to a local sexual assault service provider in your area. Trained staff can provide confidential support.

COMING SOON...

SHHH...The Documentary

A truth telling documentary that confronts child sexual abuse head on. Survivors, Professional Therapist, Poets and other advocates of child sexual abuse come together to shed light on this dark topic. Seeking to raise awareness in our communities.

NOTES:

www.ingramcontent.com/pod-product-compliance
Lightning Source LLC
Chambersburg PA
CBHW072005040325

R16275500001B/R162755PG22859CBX00001B/1